ONWARD

The Art of Leadership

by

Mark Joseph Huckabee

TELEMACHUS PRESS

Written by Mark Joseph Huckabee; https://www.businesslessons.net/contact

Edited by Abigail Lind; abigail@abigaillind.com

Cover art by Craig Christy; Raygun Tattoo—Dana Point, California. crgunvv@me.com

Published by Telemachus Press, LLC
7652 Sawmill Road
Suite 304
Dublin, Ohio 43016
http://www.telemachuspress.com

Visit the author website:
www.businesslessons.net

Library of Congress Control Number: 2019917294

ISBN: 978-1-948046-98-5 (eBook)
ISBN: 978-1-948046-99-2 (Paperback)

CATEGORY: **SELF-HELP** / Motivational & Inspirational

Version 2019.12.02

For Judah Kincaid, *the embodiment of courage, hustle, and heart.*

A Father has never been prouder of a son.

"What is to give light must endure burning."

—Viktor Frankl

TABLE OF CONTENTS

SECTION III
SETTLE FOR EXTRAORDINARY—AND NOTHING LESS

SECTION IV
ME, YOU, AND THEM: BUILDING GREAT TEAMS

SECTION V
LIVING YOUR PRINCIPLES

SECTION VI
MANAGING AN ORGANIZATION, MANAGING YOUR LIFE

SECTION VII
CHANGE THE FRAME

ONWARD

The Art of Leadership

INTRODUCTION

Leadership.

The top trait of leaders: They never quit learning and growing. Leaders are perpetual students seeking mastery of their craft. Leadership is a life-long journey with no final destination. It is a way—the ***best*** way—to live life. You will see your hard work manifest into success not only for you, but for those around you.

I promise you: *nothing* is more gratifying.

Like any journey, the first step is the most important. Leaders boldly take that step, investing in themselves as you, through this book, are doing right now. Be proud. In seeking this knowledge, you are already a leader. That critical first step is complete.

Boss. Parent. Leader. Coach.

We are all some combination of these. Your assignment: Apply each lesson herein to each role you play. All will have a unique application. Through reflection, planning, and immediate action, you transform the lessons to concrete wins in your business, your relationships, and your life.

We move forward now—you and I together. ***Our journey begins***.

—*Mark Joseph Huckabee*

SECTION I
START STRONG:
PURPOSE AND POTENTIAL

The Ice Bowl: Own the Moment

December 31st, 1967. Green Bay, Wisconsin.
Vince Lombardi's Green Bay Packers host Tom Landry's
Dallas Cowboys.

THE STAKES.

For the Cowboys: revenge against a Packers team that beat them in the same matchup one year before. For the Packers: an historic run for three consecutive World Championships.

Welcome to the 1967 NFL Championship Game. *Welcome to hell on earth*.

A cold front moves in far earlier and far colder than anticipated. At kickoff, the weather is -15 degrees Fahrenheit; -48 factoring in wind chill. It is not only the coldest title game ever played in the NFL, but also the coldest New Year's Eve in Green Bay history.

A marching band preparing for the halftime show are forced to cancel. Frozen woodwind instruments do not function. Brass instruments instantly freeze to the lips of performers; seven are hospitalized with hypothermia. A referee's whistle freezes to his lip and, when pulled off, pulls skin with it. Whistles are banned; referees use signals and voice commands in their place. An elderly man dies in the stadium from exposure to the elements.

The players themselves fight frostbite. Common in the hands, though par-
ticularly bad in the feet—causing toes to turn purple and nails to fall off.

THE GAME.

Conditions on the field rapidly deteriorate. With no halftime show to keep
the playing field churned, sheets of jagged ice take form. The sun descends.
The wind accelerates. The temperature drops. The field falls into shadow.

It is now -20 degrees.

After a 14-0 rampage, the Packers surrender 10 points from two turnovers.
On a halfback option play, Dallas's Dan Reeves throws a 50-yard touchdown strike to receiver Lance Rentzel.

The Cowboys now lead.

The Packers answer, driving the ball 68 yards.

First and goal.

Bart Starr hands off to Donny Anderson, desperate to punch through for
the game-winning touchdown. Anderson's feet slip as he stumbles back at
the one-yard line.

2nd and goal.

Again, Starr hands off to Anderson for the go-ahead touchdown. Again,
Anderson slips on the ice, barely securing the ball before stumbling, once
more, at the one-yard line.

3rd and goal.

The next play will be the last—*time is gone.* One yard to go in impossible
conditions.

THE MOMENT.

The Packers call a time-out. Starr runs to Lombardi on the sideline.

Starr: *"Coach, the linemen can get their footing for the Wedge, but the backs are slipping. I'm right there, I can just shuffle my feet and lunge in."*

Lombardi: *"Run it, and let's get the hell out of here."*

Starr returns to the huddle. With no intent of handing the ball off, Starr tells the team it will be a fullback run play.

The Packers offense, the Dallas Doomsday defense, the fans, and the sports world watch as Starr keeps the ball—diving head-first across the goal line—and into history.

OWN THE MOMENT.

Whether on the horizon or somewhere beyond—your moment is coming.

Three words to guide you: *courage, hustle,* and *heart. Courage* to step away from comfort toward your highest pursuit. *Hustle* to do so with swift action. *Heart* to do so with relentless resolve.

Be brave. Be bold. Be fearless.

You will deliver.

You will own the moment.

And you will shine.

"Leaders are made, they are not born. They are made by hard effort, which is the price which all of us must pay to achieve any goal that is worthwhile."
—Vince Lombardi

Fearless: The Molotov Cocktail Strategy

In World War II, civilian soldiers had no efficient means to combat enemy tanks that rolled through their cities. Standard methods: an opposing tank or enormous cannonry. The threat must be met with equal—or superior—force.

There is, however, one exception. **Meet the *Molotov Cocktail*.**

Composed of common household items, the cocktail is no more than a glass bottle filled with alcohol and the means to ignite it. When thrown into a tank's engine bay, the ensuing fire stalls the motor or suffocates those within. A tank with an open hatch fares far worse—a well-placed Molotov cocktail engulfs the crew in flames, or, detonating non-fireproofed stores of ammunition, destroys tank and crew alike.

Never has warfare seen such a tremendous ROI in sheer destructive power: a handful of common items capable of overcoming engineering's most lethal killing machine.

What the Molotov cocktail strategy *does* require: ***fearlessness***. For the fearless civilian soldier, willing to assault a tank in close quarters, the impossible became possible: Neutralizing the enemy's most destructive force with little cost and no support. It is the fearlessness, tenacity, and bravery of these citizen soldiers we will emulate.

In *every* industry reside a number of upper-echelon targets which, if ac-quired, would change the game entirely. Identify yours now—and keep them at the forefront of your mind as we proceed. Many deem conquering these intimidating, entrenched challenges impossible.

Finance provides an excellent example, but these lessons are applicable in any context, whether you are a creative bringing a bold new idea to life or a parent seeking a better relationship with your difficult-to-reach teen. We will discuss the Molotov cocktail strategy in the context of sales, but setting an ambitious goal and investing in achieving it even when success seems uncertain are *essential* to achieve the outcomes you truly want—in any enterprise, in any setting.

There are two paths for a financial broker's success: Focus exclusively on new clients from dollar one, along with the overwhelming time and atten-tion necessary to do so, or hunt multi-million dollar marquee targets. The fearless, with one critical victory, will surpass what others take **years** to accomplish.

Only the bold claim the throne.

The broker's paycheck doesn't care about the time, energy, and effort re-quired to earn an account—only the yield. The fearless don't settle for *slow, safe,* and *easy*. The fearless are big game hunters.

The fearless continue to take advantage of low-hanging opportunities, while ceaselessly hunting premium targets. Every 6 to 8 weeks they make contact: a visit, an email, a phone call, product literature; a handwritten note. The fearless don't approach victory with high hopes and optimistic feelings. They understand winning business is a *process*. It is an algorithm. High-quality touchpoints with religious consistency build critical rapport, and ultimately win the day.

Mediocre leaders fear "*the big guys*" won't work with them, that they're spo-ken for. There's a timidity—an expectation of rejection. *Why bother? One person cannot overcome a tank.* Refuse this mindset. It is a poor excuse yielding poor results. Your goal: establishing galvanizing rapport with *all* premium targets, regardless of active selling opportunities. This requires fearless tenacity.

For the small business, the right account can ensure years of success. The savvy entrepreneur will acquire a monster client *before launching*, monetizing their business from day one. Momentum and energy ensue.

So many variables fluctuate in a vendor/client relationship. The fearless know though the hatch may not be open now, *it will be*.

A competitor's entrenched position with your prospective account is not what it seems. Vendors make mistakes. Enough mistakes, and the client will **seek other solutions**. Professional relationships can dissolve; the trust broken. Offend the wrong person, and the client will **seek other solutions**. New leadership will want to price-check the market or disrupt the status quo, instructing management to identify alternatives and **seek other solutions**.

The hatch will open. *It is only a matter of time.* And who will the prospect call now? The fearless have maintained contact for *years*. Even when there was no active business opportunity, they've remained courteous and diligent. They are not just allowed in—*they are invited in*. They are welcomed with open arms.

The fearless know the "sale" happens on the eighth to tenth contact. *The relationship must be earned over time; there is no other way*. Then, when the competition are scrambling to build credibility, you are rightfully seated at the head of the table—an established advocate in a sea of newcomers.

Let mediocre competitors attack targets that are "*good enough*" and "*more realistic*." They're comfortable being comfortable. They live for immediate gain; to avoid rejection.

Not you.

The competition's timidity fails against your tenacity. You are brave, and bold, and fearless.

You understand with a top-tier prospect, there is a world to gain and nothing to lose. Assess what you're getting from them now. *Less of nothing remains nothing.* Exempt from the paradigm of risk/reward, there is no risk, and the greatest of rewards. A rare gift.

While others sit behind the lines, you storm from the trench. You light your Molotov cocktail. You are David conquering Goliath. The larger the target, the greater the reward. The grander the glory.

Victory at all costs. You are tenacious. You are relentless. **You are fearless**.

Fortis Fortuna adiuvat.

Fortune favors the bold.

Rocky: Own Your Work

"If I say it, you won't believe it … but when Rocky said it, it was
the truth."

—Sylvester Stallone

What needs to be said about *Rocky*? You have seen it. You love it. *We all do.* Let's explore the story behind the story.

~~~

March 24th, 1975. Richfield Coliseum, Ohio. *Muhammad Ali vs. Chuck Wepner.*

Wepner—against all expectations—knocks down Ali. A virtual unknown goes the distance with The Champ, fighting with unexpected fire and passion. Sylvester Stallone, an unknown actor in the crowd, is inspired. In only four days, the entire script for *Rocky* is written.

Stallone pushes onward through *very* hard times. Years roll by. Lacking the means to provide, he sells his beloved dog. After a failed audition, Stallone shares his script with the producers—who show interest.

Stallone has $106 to his name. He has learned to function in poverty, sacrificing to succeed. He will not be stopped. Finally, the tipping point: The studio offers $360,000 for the script. Success is within grasp. *Enough money to solve everything.*

But the price is too high; the offer is contingent on Stallone not playing Rocky. The studio pictures the script as a vehicle for Robert Redford, Burt Reynolds, Ryan O'Neal, or James Caan. Not an unknown. Not an un-proven. *Stallone says no.* It is his work—an extension of himself. He *is* Rocky; there will be no other.

After Stallone's relentless determination, the studio ultimately agrees. The role is his. Yet, the studio is only partially vested in *Rocky*'s success. The film is made on a $1,075,000 budget—absurdly low at the time. To compensate, friends and family play the cast. Most scenes are shot in one take with handheld cameras. To low expectations, Rocky is finally released. Results: $225 million globally. Three Oscars, including Best Picture. Seven sequels yielding *$1.4 billion.*

Stallone's story: The fighter. The underdog. *The relentless will to win.*

Rocky's story: The fighter. The underdog. *The relentless will to win.*

~~~

Own your work.

Rocky is everything it is because the man behind it lived the experience: It is as much a biography as a work of fiction. The film is an extension of Stallone himself.

Own your work.

Employees: Make every task an extension of your values. Of your work ethic. Of *you*. The energy this creates is magnetic. Others are drawn to you. Everyone notices. Opportunities abound when you invest yourself fully. If this simply isn't possible in your current position, *it is time to move on*. This is your wake-up call. Find a cause worthy of your best.

Leaders: Give those in your charge room to own their work. Assign the right person to the task and set them to it. *Get out of the way.* There is a powerful upside to this. A relationship exists between micromanagement and mediocre results. Colleagues, when given room to display their skill set, knowledge, and passion create impossible results.

Step back. *Let them.*

~~~

Rocky isn't just a film—*it's a mirror.*

Watch again.

Do you see yourself there?

We all do.

Rocky represents the very best in all of us.

His lesson is this:

There is nothing you are incapable of accomplishing.

And you are the hero of this story.

The first step:

Own your work.

"If a man is called to be a street sweeper, he should sweep streets even as Michelangelo painted, or Beethoven played music, or Shakespeare wrote poetry. He should sweep streets so well that all the hosts of heaven and earth will pause to say, here lived a great streetsweeper who did his job well."

—Martin Luther King, Jr.

Jurassic Park: Ignite a Fire

Steven Spielberg's *Jurassic Park* (1993) will forever live not only as a cinematic triumph, but as a cultural touchstone.

T-Rex rampaging through the paddock fence. Her slanted pupils dilating in the beam of a child's flashlight. Her patient, terrifying search for those only feet in front of her. They, like us, are frozen in fear—a moment so immersive and visceral it stays with us forever.

Reflect—*really* reflect—on the first time you experienced this film, and specifically the T-Rex scene. The sense of awe and wonder; the terror—the unforgettable thrill. We'd never seen anything like it before, or so bold a vision so beautifully executed—*an experience so powerful no successors could ever hope to recapture its magic.* Four sequels have attempted to. All have failed.

~~~

Steve Jobs. 2007; keynote presentation.

A seminal moment in the world of business. Introducing ... *"an iPod, a phone, and an internet communicator. Are you getting it? These are not three separate devices—this is one device."* Instantly, the way we interact with technology (and each other) forever changed. We experienced Steve Jobs' gift to the world—*in an experience so powerful no successors could ever hope to recapture its magic.*

Standing on the Shoulders of Geniuses

The gold standard set by Jobs and Spielberg's first efforts cast a shadow so long that none following will ever achieve such glory. It cannot be done. When a film, technology, or any initiative is introduced with such purpose, power, and clarity, all who attempt to replicate it will fall short.

Dr. Ian Malcolm to *Jurassic Park* founder John Hammond:

"You stood on the shoulders of geniuses to accomplish something as fast as you could, and before you even knew what you had, you patented it, and packaged it, and slapped it on a plastic lunchbox, and now you're selling it, you wanna sell it."

Note the irony here: Dr. Malcolm's warning is as much a prophecy for the franchise's follow-up films as it is for the genetic manipulation he's referencing (this includes Spielberg's own *Jurassic Park II*, a film whose shortcomings Spielberg acknowledges). Follow-up *Jurassic Park* films stood on the shoulders of the initial masterpiece: an endless turnstile of inferior, forgettable, poorly packaged, and quickly sold sequels that insulted *Jurassic Park* more than they paid homage to it.

The leadership lesson is this.

Your initiative may be a product, service, promotion, event; *any* objective where impact matters. It is crucial for you to invest in your launch with the passion that you poured into the project itself. You get one first chance. You get one first impression. One.

Steve Jobs and Stephen Spielberg never have to stand on the shoulders of geniuses—*they are the geniuses*. And theirs is the example to emulate. Nail the launch of your initiative—hold nothing back. It is a mindset. It is an energy you create. Commit fully—in every way—to getting it right. Be bold, ambitious, grand; all-in.

Let the world stand in the shadow of your genius.

"There is one thing stronger than all the Armies of the world, and that is an idea whose time has come."

—Victor Hugo

To Kill a Mockingbird: Relentless Courage and The Power of Principle

Principle: A fundamental truth or proposition that serves as the foundation for a system of belief or behavior.

Regardless of the endeavor—start by defining your *guiding principles*.

~~~

To Kill a Mockingbird. Rural Alabama, the 1930's. Meet *Atticus Finch.*

A small-town lawyer with uncompromising principles. Atticus accepts the case of Tom Robinson—an African-American falsely accused of assaulting a white woman. In a culture entrenched in racial inequality and segregation, Atticus defends Tom knowing not only could this jeopardize his career—but also his and his family's safety.

Atticus is willing to be the center of a maelstrom to live his principles. Equality. Justice. And *relentless courage* to fight for them. When asked to take Tom's case, Atticus does so without a moment's hesitation. For a man living by predefined principles, fighting for Tom wasn't a question to consider, but a necessary action for a critical cause.

Author Harper Lee, notoriously absent from the public eye, gave only one interview regarding *To Kill a Mockingbird* (which became one of her last interviews entirely). Then and now—her message, depicted through the themes in her book, resonates. After a successful book launch, film production began, with Lee advising. She spoke proudly of the feeling on set, with cast and crew entirely absorbed in the film's message of social injustice and inequality. Her passion influenced every facet of the production, fueling an atmosphere committed to the project's guiding principle.

> *"Real courage is when you know you're licked before you begin, but you begin anyway and see it through no matter what."*
>
> —Harper Lee

~~~

1. Lee believed in the principles of equality, and justice, and relentless courage *regardless of the stakes.*

This inspired her to action.

2. Lee wrote a book whose protagonist embodies the values of equality, and justice, and relentless courage *regardless of the stakes.*

This inspired Universal Pictures to action.

3. Lee's passion on set fueled a film production team—*to a degree never before seen in cinema*—to fully invest in an ethos of equality, and justice, and relentless courage *regardless of the stakes.*

This inspired the movie crew to action.

4. The crew's passion created a film so powerful that it remains a pillar in the continued fight for equality, justice, and relentless courage *regardless of the stakes.*

This inspired the world to action.

~~~

Let's examine the process: Step four, the ultimate outcome, *required every step before it.*

Often the task seems insurmountable. This is the nature of the greatest aspirations. Do not despair thinking your actions don't matter; your contribution doesn't count. Harper Lee's first action—*the very first word itself*—didn't change the world alone. However, it was the catalyst for a chain of events resulting in a cultural phenomenon.

There are no meaningless actions when decisions are based on principle. The culmination of countless efforts—of *every* scope and size—leads to the critical tipping point for change. The larger the boulder, the more effort necessary to make it move. You don't have to see an immediate result to know you are making a difference.

You are.

What are your guiding principles? Here and now—say them. Define them. Breath them into life; they are your compass. You'll be amazed how easy tough decisions are when based on guiding principles that you have already defined.

The test of your principles is coming. The path to which those principles point may seem unnavigable. The goal may seem unattainable. *The relentless courage to conquer them is within you.* The first step is the hardest.

Take it.

> *"It is only through labor and painful effort, by grim energy and resolute courage, that we move on to better things."*
> —Theodore Roosevelt

Black Panther: The Power of Purpose

A story is often underwhelming when overhyped. We are disappointed not due to the story itself—but rather due to the expectations that insist we'll be spellbound.

Enter *Black Panther*.

This film is a love letter to all of us. Art is power—capable of inducing change, and capable of creating awareness where ignorance exists. Race, gender, ethics, equality, social responsibility, the demons we create, the demons we become—all are addressed here. *Black Panther* is an important film well deserving of its hype, with powerful themes affecting a global audience.

You ***must*** see this film—it is the crown jewel of the Marvel Cinematic Universe and merits full immersion. The purpose of this film isn't to entertain you. The purpose is to challenge you. *Black Panther* delivers on its bold promise.

The leadership lesson is this.

It's not what you sell—it's your organization's *purpose* that matters. *Black Panther* doesn't succeed because of surface-level factors—it succeeds because of powerful themes and a critical message—its *purpose*. The film speaks to the very best within us.

The product or service you provide isn't an end unto itself. Your competition can likely do what you do at a superficial level; a global economy has flattened the market. The best leadership organizations identify the need they meet, and make serving that need their purpose. Purpose transcends products. Purpose transcends technology. Purpose is the grand vision of what you bring to the table; your unique voice in a saturated field.

Studies show a millennial shift towards *brand meaning* over *brand offering.* Tap into this. Companies such as Better World Books and People Water donate on a per-purchase basis; Amazon offers a unique approach through its *AmazonSmile* program—a donation of proceeds going directly to a charity *of the purchaser's choice.* Through these brands, consumers are empowered to make a difference.

Show me an organization committed to my cause, sharing my values, changing the nature of their offering to the mutual gain of a shared higher purpose, and I will show you brand loyalty. You aren't fighting for your cause alone, dear client. *We are fighting alongside you.*

The sets, scenery, and action sequences of *Black Panther* are typical fare from the Marvel Cinematic Universe. They are not what makes *Black Panther* transcend the action film genre. It's the purpose of the underlying story that resonates so powerfully—just as it is your purpose that will determine your success or failure.

Forget products. What does your brand *mean?*

Define your organization's purpose; *Pursue that purpose relentlessly.*

> *"As far as we can discern, the sole purpose of human existence is to kindle a light in the darkness of mere being."*
>
> —Carl Jung

SECTION II
THE "HOW" OF LEADERSHIP

Ledger's Lesson:
On Preparation and the Will to Win

Impossibly good. There's no other way to describe Heath Ledger in *The Dark Knight*. Rarely is a performance so memorable. Haunting, chilling, evocative; *timeless*. Few need revisit the film to recall the experience.

In one word, how did Ledger accomplish this?

Preparation.

Committed to every facet of his role, Ledger spent weeks in character before filming began. He *became* the Joker. Channeling those who played the role before him, along with his own influences, Ledger created an in-character diary. Even on set, he developed signature touches (face paint applied by himself and caked under his fingernails) that added endless layers of verisimilitude.

Before the cameras rolled, his preparation never ceased on set. Before filming the hospital scene between the Joker and Harvey Dent, Ledger stood in the corner moving, mumbling, and speaking to himself in character for a full hour. No one called "action;" when Ledger was ready, he simply walked over and the scene began. The result: a brief dialogue on the nature of chaos seamlessly executed through unwavering preparation.

Down to the most minute detail, Ledger studied, embraced, and mastered his role.

The leadership lesson is this.

Success is not an action.

Success is a result.

Preparation is the action.

How much do you know about your offering? The competitive landscape? Are you a student of your craft, endlessly committed to learning, adapting, evolving? Adding value to clients and colleagues through a fierce determination to master every facet?

Are you a thought leader in your industry? An influencer? A tastemaker? In your industry, someone is all of those things. Their success is earned. They deserve to win.

Being the best is on *you*. Winning is on *you*. Hit the grindstone hard. Hit the grindstone now. Hit the grindstone every single day. If unprepared or uninvested, expect mediocrity. Anticipate failure. There are no shortcuts. There are no victims of results—only victims desperate to harvest a crop they never planted, never realizing their desperation is self-inflicted.

Winning is preparation. It is a decision.

Decide.

> *"Practice makes perfect. After a long time of practicing, our work will become natural, skillful, swift, and steady."*
>
> —Bruce Lee

Benjamin Franklin: Find a Way

Boston, 1722.

16-year-old Benjamin Franklin is an aspiring writer. He begins an apprenticeship in his older brother's print shop composing types, completing sheets, and delivering *The New England Courant* around town. He is honing his mastery of writing, but his brother James—the paper's editor as well as its printer—does not yet deem his material publishable.

The technical elements of printing are not enough. Young Benjamin Franklin doesn't dream of mastering the semantics of printed words—he desires to craft the words himself. He must *find a way*.

Help arrives in the form of Mrs. Silence Dogood, an anonymous contributor to *The New England Courant*. A silent benefactor known only to Benjamin Franklin. Silence Dogood's stories captivate Boston. She is born while the Dogood's emigrate from London to New England. Her father rushes above the deck to share, in triumphant jubilation, the wonderful news of her birth. Tragically, a rogue wave strikes at the same moment. He is swept out to sea—forever lost to the Dogood family.

Silence reflects on this darkest of days:

> *"Thus was the first Day which I saw, the last that was seen by my Father; and thus was my disconsolate Mother at once made both a Parent and a Widow."*
>
> —Silence Dogood

Tragedy redefined.

Silence's anonymous letters are a sensation. She mocks the conceit of Harvard students. She is critical of Boston's affinity for drinking, and the fashions of the day. She lampoons the tendency of New Englanders to discount an opinion until confirming they find the source agreeable. In a society where lambasting the upper class is taboo, Silence holds nothing back.

Boston loves her. Spellbound suitors write the newspaper, offering Silence their hand in marriage. Six months later, Silence's letters stop. The collective heart of Boston is broken.

A distraught James Franklin, via the *New England Courant:*

> *"If any Person ... will give a true Account of Mrs. Silence Dogood, whether Dead or alive, Married or unmarried, in Town or Country, ... they shall have Thanks for their Pains."*

With Boston in a fever pitch for answers, Silence Dogood reveals herself. "She" was none other than 16-year-old Benjamin Franklin. It had all been a farce. He himself wrote the letters, slipping them under the door to his brother James—who, due to a bitter rivalry, never intended to print Benjamin's work. Boston was delighted with the revelation. Being duped in such a manner proved a tremendous amusement.

Ultimately, Benjamin Franklin becomes the most famous American of his time. The path he was given would not have gotten him to his destination. *He had to find another way.* For Benjamin Franklin, Silence Dogood was the answer.

~~~

Let us look to ourselves.

Ponder that "unattainable" goal, out there, seemingly beyond reach on the distant horizon. There's likely no well-worn path from you to it. The best goals require you forge one. Look for another angle. Look from another direction. Chart a different path. It can be done. *It is within you to do so.*

Find a way.

"There are many ways of going forward, but only one way of standing still."
—Franklin D. Roosevelt

A Quiet Place: The Art of Silence

Dear leader:

Stop talking.

~~~

For this iteration of the Hollywood monster movie, it is **sound** that makes you prey. The movie is thrilling, although it requires a healthy dose of *suspension of disbelief.*

Case Study.

Reflect, for a moment, on the current human condition. As a species, we have unraveled the mysteries of the cosmos. We have traveled to other planets, even into interstellar space—beyond the confining gravitational pull now confirmed, though once only theorized, of Copernican heliocentrism. We've identified the double helix structure of deoxyribonucleic acid, broadening our knowledge of the haploid human genome sequence, its 23 chromosomes, 20,000 unique genes, and 3.1 billion base pairs—removing the veil from conditions such as peripheral neurofibromatosis. We've mastered the controversial language of particle physics theory, confirming the hypothesized Higgs boson particle which, indeed, *is* a natural product of quantum excitation.

Enter *A Quiet Place.*

In spite of these overwhelming technological advances, and countless others, our species is brought to its knees by a plagiarized version of a *Stranger Things* Demogorgon. Our titular monster has the most heinous, vile ability of all: hearing things really, really well. Never have ears been used to such sinister ends. *Never have they been so terrifying.*

How can humanity possibly be saved from the brink of annihilation? The answer, it seems, was right there all along:

An eight-year old with a hearing aid and a RadioShack walkie-talkie. Combining these two groundbreaking technologies, a child defeats humanity's greatest foe. A monster with highly tuned hearing is sensitive to high-pitched noises? *Seven billion other people couldn't figure this out?*

The leadership lesson is this.

Re-read the *human condition* "case study" above. All of it. Whoever you are, whatever your industry, whatever you're offering: That rambling jargon is what you sound like when barreling, blindly and at full speed, into your "pitch."

Post-It note this phrase, and review it before every client interaction:

Persuasion is not TELLING what is important—it is DISCOVERING what is important.

You *must* start with an understanding of the prospect's needs and expectations. Don't overthink this: ask simple, direct questions:

> *What is **your** goal?*
>
> *What is most important to **you**?*
>
> *How will **you** choose a vendor?*
>
> *How will **you** define success?*

It's about *them*. Ask questions. Seek understanding. Shut up. *Listen*.

The road map for your presentation starts with addressing the prospect's major needs. Ask, and they shall be given. Persuasion starts with understanding—not preaching. As eager as you are to speak, they are to be heard. Only after their needs are satisfied by your solution should additional *features/advantages/benefits* arise.

Many leaders have a natural inclination to communicate, present, and share a genuine enthusiasm for their offering. Everyone enjoys demonstrating their talents and skill set. You *must* fight the inclination to present first. Like those in *A Quiet Place*, you maintain religious silence. You are a detective, seeking an understanding of other's needs. You ask. You listen. You discover *their* roadmap. *Then* you speak.

Listen, learn, understand. Start your presentation from *A Quiet Place*.

"We have two ears and one mouth so that we can listen twice as much as we speak."

—Epictetus

The Art of Conversation

"He is fluent in all languages, including three that *he* only speaks."
—*The Most Interesting Man in the World*

Friends, family, colleagues. So many different people. *So many different roles.* Juggling and reconciling each—especially in settings when your different circles encounter each other—can feel overwhelming.

A powerful solution exists. Building rapport is a rare example of a universal formula speaking to a universal truth. Everyone's favorite subject: *themselves.* The most interesting person in the room is the one asking thoughtful questions, finding out what is important to others, using that information to ask *more* thoughtful questions, and has a natural curiosity about *who this person is.*

Most people in a conversation drone on about themselves, unconsciously seeking to impress. Do not do this. You do not ask yes or no questions, which shut a conversation down immediately. You ask open-ended questions that invite discussion.

Commit this critical point to memory:

**The most interesting person in the room is the one
most interested in others.**

Discover them. They will feel more connected with you, more understood—their individuality truly appreciated. Magnetic rapport is established. *Words are common.* Everyone can actively speak. It is the rare conversationalist who actively listens.

You are now one of them.

"It was impossible to get a conversation going, everybody was talking too much."

—Yogi Berra

Ayn Rand: The Power of Story

Only one book discusses Ayn Rand without discussing politics. *You are reading it.*

~~~

Assignment: Philosophy 101. Choose any philosopher below; spend ten minutes pondering the key points of their philosophy:

Socrates. Kant. Descartes. Aquinas. Hume. Sartre. Rousseau. Spinoza. Locke. Camus. Epicurus. Heidegger. Hobbes. Voltaire. Kierkegaard. Wollstonecraft. Berkeley. Adorno. Thoreau. Abelard. Haraway. Chomsky. Dewey. Levinas. Lyotard. Hobbes. Augustine. Beauvoir. Schopenhauer.

Some recalled vaguely; others forgotten entirely. The question: Why are their works disproportionately forgettable? It's not because of what *is* in their writing—*it's because of what isn't:*

STORY.

We are wired for story. Stories are teaching tools. Stories model values. Stories shape the future through the lessons of the past. Stories are easily recalled and always remembered. Stories are persuasion's most powerful resource.

Case study: Ayn Rand. *Atlas Shrugged; The Fountainhead; Anthem.* All fiction novels written by a philosopher who understands the maxim *show, do not tell*: *"A technique used in various kinds of texts to allow the reader to experience the story through action, words, thoughts, senses, and feelings rather than through the author's exposition, summarization, and description."*

Ayn Rand presents her Philosophy, *Objectivism,* in action through fiction novels. She *shows* the effects of her beliefs. Why is her philosophy so memorable? The tenets of her philosophy are presented through the power of story. Regardless of one's opinion of Ayn Rand's work, a reader's understanding—and recollection—of *Objectivism* is unmatched among her contemporaries. Philosophers gladly *tell*—Ayn Rand *shows*. Tell; we'll forget. Show—we never do.

> *"The question isn't who is going to let me; it's who is going to stop me."*
>
> —Ayn Rand

The leadership lesson is this.

STOP SELLING DATA.

Data alone: boring; forgettable. Uninteresting and *more of the same.* It doesn't matter how compelling the analytics of your proposition are. In a competitive field crowded with binary zeroes and ones, your data set is lost in the mix.

STORY IS POWER.

To the insurance agent: Don't sell the statistics about your firm's "best in class" service; tell a story of how you personally assisted a client—*just like them*—in a time of crisis.

To the nonprofit organization: Don't dazzle us with numbers and statistics—tell a story of the profound impact a *specific family* experienced through the nonprofit's work.

To the pharmaceutical representative: Tell a story of the patient type who benefits most from your offering. When the doctor sees the patient whose profile matches your narrative, recollection of story will compel prescription behavior far more than the cold statistics of a package insert.

Present a memorable case study. *Every time.* This is your role: Create compelling stories that connect to your cause at a personal level. We love stories. We loathe statistics.

In a crowded field of philosophers, Ayn Rand doesn't stand out because of the "rightness" of her views—*it is the presentation of her views through story.* Story is the greatest weapon of the effective leader. Take your proposition and craft a compelling, memorable narrative around it.

Persuade through story.

"Inside each of us is a natural born storyteller just waiting to be released."
—Robin Moore

Star Wars: The Critical Role of Communication

Solo: A Star Wars Story. Strong with The Force, this one is not. Hopefully *Solo's* title is prophetic. If a sequel is made, there may not be a Galaxy left to save.

No revealing spoilers—nothing is memorable enough to recall. Whether an ardent fan of the Star Wars canon or a recent convert to the franchise, prepare to be equally disappointed. As Master Yoda teaches, "Do or do not—there is no try."

This film does not.

Complementary components—wardrobe, acting, lighting—come together to embody high-quality filmmaking. While each are distinct entities within a film, they function as individual components of a stylized whole.

If the masochist within you dares to suffer through this movie, follow the wardrobe changes of Emilia Clarke's *Qi'ra*. These costumes are more likely to be found in *Breakfast at Tiffany's* than in a galaxy far, far away. Each ensemble appears to have come from the bargain bin at Audrey Hepburn's rummage sale. *Wardrobe Grade: F-*

Next up: Acting. When a prequel revisits characters doing just fine in future films, the magic is stolen. Stakes are lowered, outcomes predictable. The problem: Our cast seems fully aware that the magic is gone, and it shows in their acting. There's no convincing sense of urgency, tangible consequences, or imminent danger in these performances.

Despite non-stop action, blood, sweat, and tears are uniformly absent. With scant character development, our cast is given little to work with. It shows. We are barraged with countless scenes where death is "imminent"—an apparently appropriate time for witty banter and sarcastic one-liners. *Acting Grade: F-*

Lighting. This is the unforgivable sin. The film's lighting does nothing to serve the story, standing in depressing contrast to the (attempted) popcorn thrills onscreen. From beginning to end, a washed-out palette of dull grey and dirt suffocate every scene. There's no break from it.

Faces are unlit; characters are shadowed silhouettes against a glaring back-light. This style is more appropriate for a gritty noir piece or a World War I documentary. It does not work here. Ultimately, it makes no difference: Well-lit or not, this movie sucks. *Lighting Grade: F-*

Wardrobe. Acting. Lighting. None of these three departments appear to have synchronized with each other. Each component fails within itself, but compounded together? They are exponentially worse. Two wrongs don't make a right. *Three* wrongs? Disaster.

The leadership lesson is this.

Uncoordinated components dismantle your collective effort. The gears will not fit. It is critical that all contributors serve a single, guiding principle— *and do not waver.* Different roads? Yes. But all must end at the same location. All must steer toward the goal the entire way there.

The solution is surprisingly simple.

Communicate.

Include all stakeholders, define the objective, plan accordingly; meet early and meet often. *Make sure all contributors steer toward a single goal.*

Communicate.

Do so with relentless frequency. A modest misfire in only one component of a project can cripple the outcome. *Make sure all contributors steer toward a single goal.*

Communicate.

Demand (and accept) honest dialogue and open feedback; critical course correctors for a unified goal and team cohesion. *Make sure all contributors steer toward a single goal.* The result of not doing so? *The Solo effect:* a collaborative effort where none make an effort to collaborate.

Heed the warning.

> *"The single biggest problem in communication is the illusion that it has taken place."*
>
> —George Bernard Shaw

Melville, Bartleby, and When to Say No

New York City, 1819.

Herman Melville is born into a wealthy, influential family. His is a life of privilege until his father passes when Melville is 12. With his passing, the truth is revealed: The family resources are completely gone. The family is ruined. A 12-year-old Melville quits school to support his now impoverished family. His formal education is over. Many hard years later, and after five years at sea, Melville's writing career booms. His stories of seafaring adventures are a commercial success.

In 1851, *Moby-Dick* is released. The result: *critical and commercial failure*. It was not until long after Melville's passing that readers began to recognize *Moby-Dick* as his magnum opus.

Melville hates where his career is. He doesn't enjoy writing commercial (and profitable) literature; his preferred style—more philosophical and sophisticated—proves to be a commercial disaster. Coming from poverty, Melville *must* continue to write stories for a paying audience.

"Bartleby, the Scrivener: A Story of Wall Street"

Enter "Bartleby," a two-part short story published in November and December of 1853. Bartleby is hired by a Manhattan attorney, initially working hard. Then, apathy sets in. Bartleby responds to any request with the phrase *"I would prefer not to."* The task doesn't matter—he prefers not to do it. As suits his preference, Bartleby won't leave the building when his employer relocates. He dies in prison after (quite politely) preferring not to eat.

The book is a success. Melville's "Bartleby" delivers not only a commercial victory (for "*them*"), but a philosophical masterpiece (for *him*). Both objectives are accomplished. "Bartleby" is now an iconic piece of American literature. Few stories support so many philosophical interpretations in a single book—making the work a powerful return to Melville's original intent of a thought-provoking narrative.

Buckle up; here are some critical interpretations of "Bartleby," verbatim:

The book rejects the ideal of American Romanticism. The book is a searing indictment of the oppressive, soul-crushing nature of capitalist society. The book is a precursor to the absurdist literature movement. The book boldly reveals the true nature, and consequences, of clinical depression. The book is an anthem for civil disobedience. The book models transcendence and enlightenment. The book stands as a metaphor—an insurmountable wall in the American socio-economic system; a Marxist parable for the despair and malaise of an overworked underclass. The book is an allegory for Melville's psyche, and his suppressed aspirations of freedom through isolation.

Yes, these are all actual literary themes addressed in Melville's work. Credible ones? *To each their own.* For an author aiming to incite philosophic conversations, "Bartleby" was clearly a tremendous success.

There's a powerful lesson within Melville's pages. What is not questioned is the example Bartleby embodies: *the power of saying* **NO.** Simply, he will not be taken advantage of.

The leadership lesson is this.

You too must know when—and how—to say **NO.** Others will gladly take your work (and your time) for granted. Do not let them. Say **NO** when overwhelmed. Colleagues who always expect—and get—a *yes* do not ever stop asking for more. The requests will only come more frequently.

How would they know to stop? If you have said nothing, you have trained them to keep asking. Perhaps they don't understand the scope of your current work. Or understand their responsibilities versus yours. Or they are simply comfortable taking advantage of you. You must establish precedent by saying **NO**.

Explain your NO directly.

Be candid with the manager who won't quit piling it on. Explain that to start a new project, others must be deprioritized. This begins a realistic discussion of what the pressing projects are, any course corrections needed, and the time required to complete active projects without compromising quality. A good manager will appreciate your candor—and respect you for establishing boundaries.

As for the colleague who won't quit asking—go with a hard **NO**. Say yes—even once—and prepare to be asked forever. Do not allow this. Respond directly. *"That is your responsibility—not mine—and what you are paid to do."* If they ask again—have them email their request in writing. Email holds the requester responsible for the request. There's no "explaining away" an email—it is a document stating what one employee asks of another. It is permanent. It can be reviewed and discussed with appropriate management. Demand this email before questionable work is even considered.

Be polite and professional, yet firm: *My work is my responsibility; yours is yours. When it comes to doing your job for you,* **I would prefer not to.**

> *"Learn to say no in situations where saying no can be difficult, where it could mean getting fired. Say no anyway, because it could lead you to greater opportunities."*
>
> —Samuel Dash

Zombies and the
Downside of Technology

It's a great time to be human. We're connected, protected. Communication, travel—once formidable challenges—are conquered. Boundless advances in science and medicine have reshaped our world. However, such prosperity has a downside—and a chilling one. We've lost sight of the greatest danger of all.

Zombies.

By my estimate, zombies don't need to breathe, and while we're up here worrying about the threat from the surface or beyond, no one has thought about the deep, unexplored trenches of our oceans. My hypothesis: Zombies are down there. *And thriving.* A booming metropolis of the un-dead. Hospitals and healthcare. Education. Houses of worship. A judicial system—fair and just for all. And they know about us. Perhaps some are among us even now. Planning their zombie apocalypse.

Facebook. Instagram. LinkedIn. Pinterest. Etsy. *The very tools that will destroy us*. With the ability to instantly connect at a mass level, we are doomed. Zombies will organize and exploit the advantages of our digital age. Ponder this: through the magic of social media, coordinating a zombie horde will require almost *no* effort. A once meandering, disorganized affair will now be streamlined and, ultimately, quite practical.

Add to this toxic marriage of zombies and social media *the automated car*. While we herald a new dawn of automated transportation at affordable prices, a self-driving car will soon be *very* economical. I cannot speak to the zombies' form of currency, but even with the most modest exchange rate, the majority should be able to afford one. With push-of-a-button, autonomous navigation, a zombie needn't learn the mechanics of operating a vehicle. The car will safely deliver them to ground zero.

The time to prepare is *now*. Be practical. Dig a bunker. Pack it with dry goods and plenty of munitions. Train your children in marksmanship and guerilla warfare tactics—*while there's still time*.

~~~

There is a grand irony to our obsession with zombie culture. The internet. Social media. Email. Cell phones. All of it—these pseudo-communication tools rob of us of authentic interaction. The world can be on fire, and we're texting. Entirely oblivious. Aimlessly wandering, insatiably craving the next social media post.

We've become the very monsters we fear. **We are now the zombies**.

A family staying connected through Facebook is a great thing—unless that digital connection becomes a substitute for face-to-face interaction. Headphones are great, but now, we roam around in an urban trance oblivious to those around us. Computers are great, but now, instead of enjoying the outdoors and exercising, we're sitting indoors and eating. Email is great, but now, instead of talking to a colleague fifteen feet away, we email them.

Let's fight this trend. *Every time you can—talk in person*. Make it a conversation. Value authentic connection over digital convenience. This is especially true for *tough* discussions. For topics deemed sensitive, constructive criticism, or otherwise "bad news." Emails are cold. Indifferent. Impersonal. Emails do not relay tone—which, in communication, is *far* more important than verbiage.

Authentic relationships require authentic interaction.

It is an error of leadership not discussing hard truths in person; to relay disappointing news through email. The colleague, friend, or family member will feel you are indifferent and unconcerned. Your *intentions* mean nothing. Have you received—or written—a well-intentioned email perceived as uncaring? The problem isn't what you said—*it's the tone-deaf platform you chose to communicate through*. Cat posters are fine over email. Challenging discussions are not. If it's even slightly questionable, discuss it in person.

Our survival depends on it. When zombies destroy the power grid, there won't be any form of digital media—only traditional communication. Practice the art of authentic interaction.

Hone these skills while there's still time.

> *"If we continue to develop our technology without wisdom or prudence,*
> *our servant may prove to be our executioner."*
>
> —Omar Bradley (General, US Army)

Cloverfield: Defy Expectations

There is a reason many movies evoke similar emotions—and generally *feel* the same. As viewers we often sense this, knowing without knowing that there is a pattern—a formula followed with the same feel-good results. Our protagonist wrestles with an internal struggle, and over the course of the story, overcomes his or her flaw—emerging as a self-actualized person ready to change the world.

This universal monomyth formula, called **the Hero's Journey** (first chronicled in Joseph Campbell's *The Hero with 1,000 Faces*), is so powerful it has emerged in cultures that are entirely removed from one another. Story structures, like living organisms, compete for resources (in this case, the limited attention of an audience). The story forms that resonate emerge dominant; the others fall away.

The power of the monomyth resonates universally, and thus is not culture-specific, but rather impactful for all cultures at all times. The format inspires tangible, real-world results. If you want to capture hearts and minds, the monomyth is the time-tested formula.

However, even the strongest forms can be exhausted.

Enter *Cloverfield*.

Many viewers find *Cloverfield* unsettling—and for good reason. The film defies classic storytelling, ignoring the predictable monomyth structure. The first act deceives us, launching in a direction that is entirely disconnected from what transpires. What seems like a coming-of-age romantic comedy dissolves into pandemonium. Well into the story, seemingly out of no-where, a monster attacks New York City.

The film is haunted by an ending where nothing is resolved, and (with the exception of Lily) none survive. The traditional "*I love you*" finale does occur—but, like all scenes before it, the sentiment is instantly negated and rendered completely meaningless in the film's final moments. Our hero and heroine do not make it out alive.

Love, strength of character, willpower, and the relentless drive of the hu-man spirit mean *nothing* against so powerful a force as our monster. Our expectation of a feel-good ending is betrayed. With none of the traditional story beats of the monomyth, *Cloverfield* is entirely—and refreshingly—unique.

Other convention-defying elements of Cloverfield deserve praise. Production was greenlit with the utmost secrecy; no details leaked. Even the first trailer fed the mystery—*the movie's title was left unrevealed*. The story's big-gest question (*where is our monster from?*) appears to be left unanswered.

However, it is. Rewatch the final scene in frame-by-frame slow motion—our hero and heroine on a Coney Island Ferris wheel. The camera pans out to the ocean; a large boat is seen on the horizon. Like a meteor, our mon-ster descends from the sky into the ocean. This is so fine a detail that only the most discerning viewer will find it; a tremendous reward hidden in plain sight. Another expectation-defying masterstroke.

Had the traditional monomyth remained unchallenged, *Cloverfield* would not be what it is.

The leadership lesson is this.

During your project, product, or service's **beta phase** (when you are fire-testing initial concepts), *don't be afraid to defy traditional boundaries.*

This truth holds in all contexts: To be great, artists must think beyond the conventions of their medium. Parents who argue with their teens over the same topic day in and day out need to adopt a different perspective on the problem. That means thinking creatively before embarking on a new project; before initiating the conversation that will change your relationships.

You **do not** start breaking boundaries in the middle of the game—you do it in the game *planning* phase—*precisely* the time to do so. Entertain exotic concepts. Trial, error, fresh ideas, and new perspectives reward the bold. Think of beta testing as a piano—there are countless keys available; each unique. How easy it is to sit and play the same note over and over, unaware—or unwilling—to step outside of what is familiar, what is comfortable, what is known.

Consultants help break the paradigm with fresh perspectives. Hire one.

In business, tap down the organizational chart as well; colleagues working directly with your customers are a treasure trove of fresh concepts. These colleagues have the best understanding of the end user's experience, and the pros and cons therein. Treat them as advocates for your client's needs. Value their ideas. Their voice matters.

Challenge your organization. Challenge yourself. *Defy expectations.* Step outside of traditional (and self-imposed) boundaries. The same pattern yields the same outcome.

Break the pattern.

> *"I have an almost complete disregard of precedent, and a faith in the possibility of something better. It irritates me to be told how things have always been done. I defy the tyranny of precedent. I go for anything new that might improve the past."*
>
> —Clara Barton

Pixar: The Power of Brand Equity

Scene:

It is kids' movie night. You're bracing for the storm.

Prepare for, at best, a 90-minute time sink of what could have been a great evening; at worst, a $90 money sink at the theater. Regardless, it is likely your faith in humanity will be completely destroyed by the experience. None should be subjected to this.

However, there is one exception. **Pixar.** More specifically—*anything* Pixar. The studio delivers such high quality that, when any upcoming release is in the works, we anticipate a masterpiece with themes transcending the children's film genre. Or any film genre, for that matter. Pixar has rightfully earned this reputation.

Brand equity:

"The commercial value that derives from consumer perception of the brand name of a particular product or service, rather than from the product or service itself."

Case study.

The first draft of *Toy Story 2* was written for direct-to-video production. The script was too short for feature-length release, with attempts to lengthen the script unsuccessful. Extensive rewrites ensued.

Pixar would not compromise.

Pixar got to work on the updated version. With nine months till deadline, the team watched *Toy Story 2*'s development reels. The film *still* wasn't working.

Pixar would not compromise.

Pixar informed Disney the film would not make deadline. All or nothing—no concessions made for mediocrity. *Pixar would not compromise.* Disney held legal control over the film's completion date through contractual obligations with product licensees and marketers. The film *must* be done in 9 months. Two options for Pixar: Deliver a product they didn't believe in, or achieve the impossible: Deliver a product—done to their exemplary standards—in only nine months. In moviemaking, this is a nearly impossible feat.

Pixar would not compromise.

They bet on themselves to create a film worthy of their brand identity. For nine months, the team worked *relentlessly* to make deadline. The final product arrived on schedule. The result? Only 3 children's films have earned critical scores of 100% on the aggregator site Rotten Tomatoes:

1. *Pinocchio*
2. *Mary Poppins*
3. Appropriately, the first *Toy Story*

Three children's films. Three, ever. *Toy Story 2:* 100% critical score, earning a rightful place in the pantheon of the greatest children's films of all time. An historic achievement.

The leadership lesson is this.

Take measure of your brand equity. What is your organization's identity? Your culture, your reputation? What do your clients say about you? Your competition? Your colleagues? Are you willing—or unwilling—to compromise quality in the face of adverse circumstances? Do you live the values you espouse—*are they evident in everything you do?*

Compromise nothing, ever. *Earn it.*

Embrace the challenges of making your organization the most prestigious in your field.

~~~

Yes, it's kids' movie night. But this one will be different. It's a Pixar movie. *The Incredibles 2*, as of this writing, premieres soon. I know nothing of it. I have not seen it. Regardless, I can provide a review:

I know it will be exceptional. After all, it's Pixar. I know my children will leave the theater smiling—as will I.

Pixar delivers quality. Every film, every time. Pixar's brand equity lets viewers know that in a wasteland of children's films, this will be an exceptional experience. Do not compromise quality, ever. Pixar has earned their prestige.

I challenge you to do the same.

"You can't build a reputation on what you are going to do."

—Henry Ford

Hunter S. Thompson: Know Your Audience

Gonzo Journalism:

A highly personal writing style breaking the tightly edited confines of traditional media. Stories are given character and personality, often humorous and profane. The author stands as the protagonist—we are immersed in the story through his or her experience.

Meet the Father of Gonzo Journalism, Hunter S. Thompson. After modest early success, Thompson received national acclaim for his 1967 book *Hell's Angels: The Strange and Terrible Saga of the Outlaw Motorcycle Gangs*. Thompson's style of grit and realism captivated a national audience. He became a bastion for the underrepresented counterculture rising in 1960s America.

Hell's Angels immerses us in the true story of the notorious California motorcycle chapter. The final product is personal, genuine; *real*. We ride along with Thompson as he chronicles the authentic experience of life as a *Hell's Angel*.

Traditional journalism includes standard research and token interviews. While informative, we're given a surface-level examination in a sterile format. Gonzo Journalism bursts to life on the page. We are alongside the author, experiencing both facts and emotions. Gonzo Journalism tells the complete story. How did Thompson accomplish this? *Immersion*. Thompson spent a year with the notorious gang, living in their world. It is this level of immersion that yields so rich, complex, and compelling a story as *Hell's Angels*. Thompson's work will live forever because of it.

Those who know their stakeholders best win. A superficial understanding of your audience is *never* enough. Words and case studies are not enough. You must stand next to them. You must stand with them. You must observe. Engage. Understand. What motivates them? What are their struggles, challenges, wants, and needs? *There is no greater teacher than firsthand experience.*

Often, the most effective leaders come from the industry they currently serve. They *were* the audience that are now their stakeholders. They have a degree of insight and forethought that only come from personal experience. A leader who has lived the role they now cater to AND has premium leadership skills is *invaluable* to an organization.

Immersion. Put this principle to work. Leaders: Intern with your audience. Every new salesperson should execute this task early in their training (recall the concept of *show, don't tell*). Spend a few days not as a "representative"— but as an observer. Most clients welcome sharing their working culture. You are a student. They are your teachers.

The threefold benefits:

    —Empathy with the needs of your stakeholders and audience.

    —Understanding where your offering will make impact.

    —Unmatched rapport.

Get in their space.

Establish yourself as a welcome guest and the door will always be open. You cannot buy the impact of a positive, authentic relationship. It transcends discounts and clever marketing. It only comes from firsthand experience. It only comes from learning their world and earning their trust: A *priceless* combination for your organization; a *devastating* one for your competition.

Immersion.

You are no longer a standard leader. You are a Gonzo leader. *All-in*. No one will know your audience like you do, and it will pay off in spades. You remain relentlessly curious about their world. The more you know, the more value you add—the results will follow.

Gonzo leadership. Stop selling "at" them. ***Start growing with them***.

> *"Never treat your audience as customers, always as partners."*
>
> —James Stewart

South Pacific: On Progress and Credibility

The BBC's *South Pacific* takes a well-rendered look at the cruelty of deep-sea net fishing. Immediately following, the series then promotes line-caught fishing as an easy answer.

Fishermen throw lines, then yank; the fish fly, one at a time, 40 or more feet overhead, "mercifully" slamming onto the ship deck with blunt force. One apron-clad deckhand armed with a single club beats the fish to death before sending what remains down into the boat's hold.

We are witness to this horrendous spectacle in stunning high-definition ultra-slow motion. While the documentary series does show, powerfully and accurately, the barbarism of net fishing, it overstates the line-caught process's potential as a perfectly humane solution.

Apparently, a line-caught death is not one to mourn—*but to celebrate*. It's impossible to know exactly what a line-caught fish is thinking, though the documentary producers would have us believe:

Thank you for this privileged, humane death. Honor me, my human Brother. Honor me at your corporate fish fry. Honor me at Long John Silver's. Honor me at Captain D's. Honor me with garlic butter, and bedfellows of mixed, steamy vegetables swimming in a sea of Grandmother's coleslaw.

The leadership lesson is this.

Celebrate progress, but don't oversell marginal improvement in a desired direction. Each step toward an ultimate goal deserves recognition. A *modest* step presented as an end-all solution is a credibility killer. You will lose the trust of your clients. You will lose the respect of your colleagues. Until the endgame is reached, you have not yet arrived.

Keep fighting.

"Honesty is the first chapter of the book of wisdom."

—Thomas Jefferson

The Matrix Revolutions: Predicting Failure

I've put this off far too long. I don't think there's a piece I've dreaded writing more than this, as writing it requires re-watching the movies.

The Matrix Revolutions. This is a shit film.

> **"This is a shit film."**
>
> —Mark Joseph Huckabee

The first *Matrix*—*jaw-dropping*. The action, the pace, the brilliant—and believable—use of cutting-edge technology. Yes, there were philosophical implications, but they deftly served the story while giving us the greatest action sequences in cinema. All of this was done right.

The Matrix Reloaded … okay. Not as good. A portion of the special effects were laughable—unsuccessfully forcing CGI technology clearly not yet ready for the big screen.

Then there's *Revolutions*. The filmmakers commit the majority of the movie's two hour and nine minute runtime to answering a question no one ever asked: What is going on in the "real world" of Zion? Answer: *Who cares?*

Our cast's acting is more robotic than the machines themselves. Around halfway through, I found myself rooting for the *sentinels*, the robots tasked with eliminating the human resistance. *Please end this*, I implored them. *I still have to go to the grocery store and laundromat today—two events far more thrilling than this disaster.*

Revolutions is more interested in preaching philosophy than astonishing us. The film becomes arrogant and self-indulgent, not only for robbing us of the stunning Matrix itself—the world *within* the world we have grown to love—but drowning us in its philosophy of *free will vs. determinism*. Literally— every moment is either a fight scene, or an opulent, eloquent philosophical diatribe being preached with *far* too heavy a hand.

The filmmakers forgot their contract with the audience. When a product is introduced, there is an unspoken contract between creator and audience. For *The Matrix*, this contract included cutting-edge, believable technology and a story primarily based in "the Matrix" itself—a rich, immersive world as much a character as the cast themselves. We fell in love with the scenes where our crew are *dialed in*, understanding the "real world" scenes were necessary to serve the story—but graciously limited. The filmmakers committed to giving us what we want.

This is why *The Matrix Revolutions* sucks: The contract was broken—instead of believable, cutting-edge technology, we are presented with technology too far ahead of its time, and given a story mostly removed from the Matrix itself—the heart and soul of the franchise.

~~~

New Coke.

Between the 1940s and 1980s, Coke's market share was in steep decline. In a desperate attempt to course-correct, Coke boldly changed the recipe of its signature cola. Consider this. Coke—an American tradition *since 1886*. As much a piece of Americana as baseball, apple pie, and the white picket fence. How to fix things? *Change the formula completely.*

Coke had a contract with its audience. The formula was changed. The contract broken. Customers were furious; over 40,000 letters and calls flooded the company. Instead of *growth of a proven platform through innovation*, Coke abandoned its core competency entirely.

Coke broke its contract with lifelong customers. Do not re-pour the foundation of a product that has become an American Institution. Your customers will hate you for it. *The Matrix Revolutions* broke its contract with its audience. Do not re-pour the foundation of a movie that has become an American institution. Your audience will hate you for it. Your task is this: innovation *without* compromising your core competency; *without* breaking the contract that keeps your customers with you.

While *Revolutions* was the last in a trilogy and thus had no chance to course-correct, Coke did. The old formula was brought back, breathing new life into a rich tradition. Sales instantly boomed.

Cherry Coke. Also introduced in 1985, but instead of changing a winning formula, Cherry Coke innovated on a proven concept. Cherry Coke was—and remains—a huge hit.

The leadership lesson is this.

What are your organization's core competencies? The contract with your audience? What changes would stray so far from your customer's expectations they would feel abandoned entirely?

Yes- explore bold concepts in the new product/service beta phase where we appropriately *defy expectations*. This is where innovation is born. It is *not* done by burning the rest of what's working to the ground, with a gambler's all-in faith that this new thing *just might work out*. You do not abandon your core business because the skunkworks department has, what may be, a promising concept. You must maintain the foundation of the contract with your customers *while* innovating. Build on what is proven. Build on what works.

The Matrix Revolutions sucks. So does a revolution abandoning your core identity entirely. In the world of business,

Evolution is far more important than revolution.

"The moment you give up your principles, and your values, you are dead, your culture is dead, your civilization is dead. Period."
—Oriana Fallaci

Hire Right: 50 Shades of No Chemistry

For the sake of research—*and for the sake of research only*—I took it upon my-
self to watch this movie. There I stood, for you, dear reader, in line at
Target—a copy of *50 Shades of Grey* discreetly tucked between a $7.99
Henley and a box of Frosted Flakes.

Let's get right into this. A titillating concept ruined by a lead actor and act-
ress who, on a scale from 0 to 10, have chemistry of -6. It is a film more
boring—and somehow *less* "erotic"—than watching paint dry. Critics agree.
With an overall score of 25%, the consensus was: disaster.

Evidence abounds. This movie required extensive reshoots; the scenes
promising passion and intimacy lacked any passion, or intimacy. The promotional tour became a public relations nightmare. *Set your expectations to
smolder.* Two professionals hired to portray a ravenous, insatiable magnetism
couldn't get sitting next to each other right. Their discomfort and dislike of
one another defined the promotional tour.

Let's call this what it is: a casting disaster. A riveting concept ruined.

The leadership lesson is this.

Add the wrong person, and whatever you gain from their expertise is lost
many times over in the overall damage to your team. Culture doesn't just
"count". *Culture is everything.* The final result is *always* measured by the effort

of the collective whole. One toxic teammate will infect every colleague and every outcome.

Here's how to get it right.

~~~

TEAM BUILDING.

Don't hire a skillset. *Hire an attitude.* Attract the right people. You can teach skills; you can hand down knowledge. *You cannot change attitude.*

Add proven performers. The greatest indicator of future success is past success. Successful people practice habits yielding optimal results in any endeavor. They will adjust to the landscape. They will learn your playbook. They will flourish.

Don't listen to what people say—*examine the results of what they've done.* Words are words; proven results are concrete. *Success breeds success.*

LOOK FOR FUNDAMENTAL MISMATCHES.

In some cases, the answer isn't obvious, or a matter of right or wrong. New members *must* fit into the working culture of your team.

Example: a new member requests to work remotely, with a team who work together daily. Or a new member thrives in a hands-on working environment, but is brought into a team who meet once a week and otherwise work remotely.

You must get this right.

The fundamental adjustment of work style may work for a time, but ultimately, you have set the new member up for failure. His or her style must match the team's; *a glove fit is critical.* Otherwise, the new member's work satisfaction and engagement will slowly corrode. They, the group, and the outcome will suffer.

NAIL THE SCREENING PROCESS.

You are looking for *attitude*. You are looking for *proven results*. Neither of these require an interrogation to identify.

If you are employing firing squad tactics to those you interview, stop. You are being interviewed as well—premium talent understand the need for a cultural match, and they will avoid any organization unworthy of their best effort.

Ask these questions:

> *What are your ambitions?*

> *What are your professional strengths and authentic professional weaknesses?*

> *What will your last three employers/references say about you?*

Then call the last three managers/references. Share what the candidate stated. Verify authenticity of facts. Gauge the demeanor of the candidate from your interactions and the feedback of the managers/references. We're looking for consistency in what the candidate, and his or her references, have to say. With high-integrity prospects, it will all align.

Combine each of these tactics. If the right candidate does not show up, you do not proceed. *Do not let impatience fuel a hiring mismatch.* You are courting disaster by doing so. Good enough isn't. *Keep hunting.*

~~~

Ultimately, *50 Shades of Grey* introduces a host of unorthodox concepts—all of which I adamantly oppose. Golf cart batteries, tire irons, and a Black & Decker pressure washer do *not* belong in the bedroom. Each scene of this abomination? Deeply upsetting to my Judeo-Christian sensibilities. This film should never be seen by anyone, ever. It is a blight on society that such garbage exists—*and shame on any who indulge in it.* I finished the film over-whelmed with shame and disgust.

And it was no better the second time I watched it.

> *"The way a team plays as a whole determines its success. You may have the greatest bunch of individual stars in the world, but if they don't play together, the club won't be worth a dime."*
>
> —Babe Ruth

Avengers: The Danger of Meaningless Consequences

Avengers: Infinity War.

Brace yourself—once launched, this one doesn't let go till the credits roll. Josh Brolin, as Thanos, gives a remarkably human performance. Thanos is a complex, multifaceted antagonist. There's far more going on here than a one-dimensional and predictable villain. The audience notes this immediately.

In the film's final act, our heroes begin dropping at a staggering rate. Each death sequence is brilliantly acted and sincerely portrayed. The problem is this: Most of these deaths are entirely meaningless. *And the audience knows it.* They'll all be back; we've seen it before. We'll see it again. Death is yet another conquerable force for our heroes. The flaw in the Marvel Cinematic Universe: Nothing is ever final, and there are no irreversible consequences.

Imagine an alternate ending to *Gladiator* after Maximus dies. After Lucilla states, "*He was a warrior of Rome—honor him,*" an elderly, grizzled Shaman descends into the arena—revealing a life-saving amulet from a parallel dimension. Within moments, Maximus is restored to full health, leading a rowdy crowd of Romans into town for a night of debauchery.

Note the problem here. If Maximus's death were reversible, *the film wouldn't work at all*. The power of the story hinges on the finality of his sacrifice. Without meaningful consequences, the power of the story is stolen.

The leadership lesson is this.

Ethics. Human Resources. Organization rules. Corporate guidelines.

There must be highly defined policies with *meaningful consequences*. Our ethics are clearly taught, their repercussions clearly defined. *Teach them religiously.* Ingrain them in the ethos of your organization.

Make a *single* exception, and you'll be making that exception for all who follow—unless you want to be sued by the next person also expecting a "free pass." *Precedent must be set.* Make the break quick and clean. It isn't easy. *It is reality.* Those who compromise ethical integrity must go.

Ethics are the linchpin of modern organizations. You *cannot* make exceptions. Careers, marriages, entire companies: We've all seen the catastrophic damage when ethics are compromised; something seemingly small and insignificant blossoming into a never-ending nightmare for all involved. Within a defined and acknowledged policy, there are no shades of grey.

Define the ethical guidelines of your organization with complete clarity. State the consequences. And most importantly:

Mean it.

"Choice of attention—to pay attention to this and ignore that—is to the inner life what choice of action is to the outer. In both cases, a man is responsible for his choice and must accept the consequences, whatever they may be."

—W. H. Auden

Sex, Politics, Religion: Don't Bring Them Where They Don't Belong

Sex. Politics. Religion. *Professional kryptonite.* Do not discuss this Holy Trinity at work. Or the hotel bar after a conference. By the water cooler. In the parking lot. Over the phone, by email, directly, indirectly—*none* of this, in ANY form, ever.

Sex. Politics. Religion. Each are defining issues to *everyone.* Each a pillar of one's identity. Whether you perceive it or not, you will alienate others. You do not have to recognize their discomfort. The person nodding politely during your diatribe is often the most offended.

Emails last forever. Relationships go south. Some colleagues leave. Some colleagues sue. Welcome to the digital age; you are being watched—*everything* stays on record.

Sex. Politics. Religion. *Keep your private beliefs private.* Keep your professional relationships professional.

There are *no* exceptions.

"The purpose of separation of church and state is to keep forever from these shores the ceaseless strife that has soaked the soil of Europe in blood for centuries."
—James Madison

300: The Alliance of Task and Skillset

300. A dramatized version of The Battle of Thermopylae during the ancient Persian Wars.

Sparta's King Leonidas refuses to kneel to the Persian God-King Xerxes. War is imminent. King Leonidas and 300 of his Royal Guard prefer dying free over living in bondage. The Spartans strategically places the battle-ground at a narrow pass between a rocky cliff and the sea; *the Hot Gates*.

This *brilliant* tactical maneuver exploits the close quarters superiority of Spartan warfare. An interlocking Spartan shield wall creates a choke point against an endless sea of Persian light infantry; the impenetrable Greek phalanx. In the confines of *the Hot Gates,* Persian numbers are meaningless. The Spartan line cannot be broken.

The mass of the Persian Army becomes a liability—so large a force requiring enormous supply lines to maintain. *The Persian Army must keep moving.* Wave after endless wave of Persian attacks fall against the Spartan line.

Against all odds, the Spartans hold out until the third day. A secret passage allows the Persians to execute an encircling maneuver. King Leonidas and the brave 300, through their sacrifice, inspire Greece to unite in war. Thousands of years later, they inspire us still.

Their legend lives forever.

The leadership lesson is this.

To assign the right positions, a coach *better* know their players damn well.
To do this, you must deeply understand the disposition of your team.
Absorbing their skillsets, learning their strengths, observing their weak-
nesses, personalities, work that actively engages them, *work that actively
disengages them*—every facet. You must align the task to those with the
strongest skillset for it.

First, deeply contemplate your endeavor; its requirements and complexities.
Entirely, and from every angle. With this deep understanding, you now pair
the *task* to those with the best *skillset* for it. King Leonidas paired the right
task (*a blockade at the Hot Gates*) to the right skillset (*the Spartan heavy infantry
phalanx*).

You must do the same.

There is a right way to do this: as important as pairing task and skillset is
how you present the new assignment. Present tasks as opportunities. Do
not play "*You get stuck with it,*" which leads to a mediocre outcome and dis-
engaged team. Make it clear: This is an opportunity to step up. To advance.
To show your best. To develop your skillset, your career; *yourself.* The benefits are twofold: increased employee engagement—and the optimal outcome. *Win/win.*

The Spartans lost the battle, but Greece ultimately won the war. Just so in
business: Aligning the right team to the right task may not guarantee a win
every single time, but it will ensure long-term victory.

The history is ancient. *The wisdom is timeless.* Leonidas's lesson:

Pair the right task with the right person—*ultimate success is yours*.

~~~

Historical note: Thermopylae was **not** a battle between two ancient super-
powers. Greece was a loose confederation of city-states constantly warring
with one another; Persia a massive Empire which, had it ultimately

conquered Greece, would likely have pressed deep into Europe. *The significance of Thermopylae was in unifying the Greek resistance.* Actual numbers vary in different retellings of the legend: The 300 Spartans were supported by 7,000 unified Greeks; the Persians who, per ancient sources, were "over a million" strong, were likely 100,000-150,000 in number.

> *"A pessimist sees the difficulty in every opportunity; an optimist sees the opportunity in every difficulty."*
>
> —Winston S. Churchill

SECTION III
SETTLE FOR EXTRAORDINARY—
AND NOTHING LESS

Dreamers, Doers, and the Difference:
Field of Dreams

"We just don't recognize life's most significant moments while they're happening. Back then I thought, 'Well, there'll be other days.' I didn't realize that was the only day."
—Doctor Archibald Graham, *Field of Dreams*

What a wonderful film. Inspiring, sincere—timeless. *Field of Dreams* challenges the viewer to not only pursue his or her greatest aspirations—but to remain steadfast in doing so against all opposition.

Ray Kinsella, played by Kevin Costner, is an Iowa corn farmer. While in the cornfields, he hears a transcendent voice, challenging him to build a baseball diamond. This vision requires sacrificing profitable farm space that is critical to Ray's livelihood. With the support of his family, Ray builds the baseball diamond. As a result, the farm goes bankrupt. Despite a generous purchase offer, Ray and his family carry on. They will see their vision through with complete faith and unwavering determination.

We, as Ray and his family, learn what the baseball diamond is about—second chances for those who have sacrificed a dream for another calling. First summoned is "Shoeless" Joe Jackson, a disgraced baseball player from the 1919 Black Sox—a team embroiled in a game-throwing scandal. Writer Terence Mann, family practitioner Doc Graham, and Ray's beloved father also answer the call—each finding the courage to face the aspirations they've abandoned. As does Ray. *As do we.*

Dreamers, Doers, and the Difference

"*Dreams.*"

Lofty aspirations we aspire to. We talk about them—even obsess over them. They are our highest calling, and for the life truly lived, they *demand* pursuit. However, so many *talk* about their aspirations; a "later-in-life" goal; an action to initiate "*when there's time.*"

These are *dreamers*. Dreamers can speak endlessly about the result they want. But how to get there? *Not certain.* Doers also speak about the result they want—*but are as aware of the process of getting there as the end goal itself.* Dreamers are often oblivious to the process their goals demand. Unaware of the steps required; waiting to get started when life "gives them room" to do so.

You are not a *dreamer.* **You are a doer.**

This is your roadmap.

> 1. What is my goal? (*Dream*)
>
> 2. What are the steps to get there? (*Process*)
>
> 3. What is needed to do so? (*Resources*)

Doers answer each of these questions with EQUAL EMPHASIS.

Doers have researched *process* with religious intensity. For doers, building the roadmap to success is an obsession. The destination is inevitable when the process is defined, each step understood, and the time and resources to do so are prioritized. Doers understand the grandest dreams require the greatest investment. They plan their work—and then get to it.

Dreamers can't speak to process. Doers can. Doers know the steps. Doers know the step they are on. Doers know the next step coming, and how to get there. In a word: *trajectory.* Dreamers talk, but progress is flat. Doers say far more through their actions—which, with relentless momentum, will collide with their ultimate goal.

Once more, the three stages.

Write each down:

    1. What is my goal? (*Dream*)

    2. What are the steps to get there? (*Process*)

    3. What is needed to do so? (*Resources*)

Answer as thoroughly as possible. Wikipedia; YouTube; LinkedIn—resources to learn the process are instantly accessible. Study them. Information that was once buried in a library, or with an expensive consultant, is now yours for the taking. There has *never* been a time in human history where so much knowledge, so thoroughly laid out, instantly accessible, at no cost, has been available. It's all there. Waiting for you.

Who has the success you aspire to? Who's blazed the trail? Go online. *Contact them.* Successful people love to share their story. Ask for their advice. Find one mentor, and you're ready to start. Find four or five, and the path forward will be brilliantly defined. Network. Get yourself established. Put social media to work for you.

Prioritize time. You aren't going to be a high-performing athlete if you aren't training. You aren't going to start a business if you aren't learning. You aren't going to be a writer unless you are writing. Get up an hour early; your *Golden Hour*. Commit that hour to your goal without allowing **any** outside interference. Not only does your *Golden Hour* establish you on the right trajectory, it energizes the rest of your day. It is invigorating. When the rest of the world is waking up, you've already invested an hour into your ultimate goal.

The destination doesn't matter if you haven't built the road. No more "talk" about dreams. We speak through actions. We are doers—devoted to the process success demands.

Your dream is just over the horizon. Waiting for you.

Go get it.

> *"All men dream, but not equally. Those who dream by night in the dusty recesses of their minds, wake in the day to find that it was vanity: but the dreamers of the day are dangerous men, for they may act on their dreams with open eyes, to make them possible."*
>
> —T. E. Lawrence

10:00 AM: The James Bond Challenge

Ian Fleming's 007 series. *14 books*. 100,000,000 copies sold. Currently, more than *half* the global population have seen at least one Bond film.

Fleming's early endeavors include journalism and military service. During World War II, he worked for Britain's Naval Intelligence Division. Tasked with overseeing the *30 Assault Unit* and *T-Force intelligence* branches, Fleming also contributed to *Operation Goldeneye* (which, fittingly, he later named his writing retreat in Jamaica). Fleming's wartime service and career as a journalist fueled the background, detail, and depth of the *James Bond* novels.

Effective art is a natural extension of the artist themselves—the passion, creativity, and indulgences of James Bond's fictional exploits grounded in Fleming's real experiences. The extravagances of James Bond were Fleming's own. This culminated in the right story at the right time: Audiences were hungry for the British spy thriller after World War II and during the Cold War era; it was a uniformly compelling topic in an unstable age.

Though greatly admired for the punch of his prose, Fleming is often underappreciated for his meticulous research and devotion to detail. He invited others to screen his manuscripts for inaccuracies, demanding complete precision in his work. This extraordinary standard formed unseen—though critical—pillars to 007's phenomenal success. The details are not luxuries. *They are mandatory.*

An extraordinary accomplishment; an extraordinary writer. More compelling than **what** Fleming accomplished is ***how***.

> *"Work expands so as to fill the time available for its completion."*
> —Parkinson's Law

Fourteen Bond novels starting at age 43; such a prolific endeavor only possible through unwavering discipline, focus, and intensity. Fleming adhered to his schedule religiously: breakfast, a morning swim, then three hours of writing—*uninterrupted*. His home's study became a sanctuary. An additional hour late in the day, writing continued.

Let's consider *Parkinson's Law* in the context of ourselves.

It is an extraordinary truth: In work and life, when constrained by schedule, we *find a way*. We conquer. We adapt our actions to the time allowed. It's the work deadline that, no matter the sacrifice, *must* be met. It's the full day of errands that, when urgency requires, are completed by mid-morning. When we absolutely have to—we do. None are immune, and most are unaware, of *the Parkinson Law's* universal truth. We only function with a sense of urgency when necessity dictates it. *We are going to shatter the paradigm.*

The 007 Challenge

Our day begins with our *Golden Hour*, that time committed—*with no excuses*—to our highest calling. The *Golden Hour* is sacred; never to be skipped, never to be viewed as a luxury. It feeds the best within us. It fuels our lives. *It is a necessity.*

Our strategy: The *Golden Hour* is complete by 007. By seven in the morning, we have invested one hour. We have laid the foundation for our day—*and our lives*—while the rest of the world is waking up.

Now, we take this further.

The 10:00 AM Challenge

At 7:00 AM, we set a timer. A three-hour countdown. We inventory the day's responsibilities and, with *Parkinson's Law* in mind, set an aggressive goal: completing everything by 10:00 AM.

The *Golden Hour* done. The day's core tasks done. And it's *ten in the morning*. Set yourself to the task. *You've got this*. As to the work itself, we divide the day's responsibilities into two categories:

1. Activity

2. Productivity

Most activity must be seen for what it is—a distraction to keep us from the truly productive actions that we do not care to do. We find things that *feel* productive; comforts that—though not core priorities, *seem* meaningful enough. We justify doing the easy stuff first. We sell, and buy, our own bullshit. Our mindset: We're going to war with *"activity."*

Write two columns: *activity* and *productivity*.

For a full week, track your standard daily actions, placing each into the appropriate column. Truly meaningful work—*productivity*—quickly announces itself.

We attack the day, finding no comfort in pseudo-productive *"tasks."* We prioritize; we execute. The heaviest lifting is always done first. Your *Golden Hour* is complete by 7:00 AM. Does 10:00 AM seem lofty for all else? *Try it*. Challenge yourself. You'll be amazed at what you're capable of as the clock ticks down.

There's no greater gift than time, which you have now given yourself in abundance. Use it effectively.

The work projects that truly matter. An early assault on tomorrow's responsibilities. Some brief, well-earned leisure. Best of all—a second *Golden Hour*—or more. Ian Fleming returned to his writer's desk for an extra hour every day. Do the same.

For each of us, there comes that wonderful moment when the day's doing is done. When, with pride in the day's accomplishments, we've earned the right to decide all that will follow.

I'll meet you there at ten.

"You've got to get up every morning with determination if you're going to go to bed with satisfaction."

—George Horace Lorimer

The Psychology of Envy/The Golden Hour

Renowned psychologist Sigmund Freud theorized that man's "*bigger is better*" obsession stems subconsciously from a fear of reproductive ... *inadequacies*. That we envy those with more procreational fortitude, equating size with power.

Meet the Argentine lake duck.

"The Argentine lake duck is small, weighing a little more than a pound and measuring around 16 inches long from head to tail. It's a stiff-tail duck, and like many species in the stiff-tail duck family, they have rather long *****es compared to their body size. Most of these birds rival human length at approximately 6 to 8 inches. The Argentine lake duck appears to be an overachiever and can have a ***** up to 17 inches long, giving them the largest ***** of any known bird."

Applying the duck's unprecedented ratio, the human male would have "equipment" measuring ten to twelve feet.

   Duck: 1

   You: 0

So, we envy the duck. **Why?**

We must deal with a hard truth: We'll never catch up to the duck. We'll never rise to the occasion. We cannot compete with such stiff competition. We will forever fall short. Understand: Regardless of the endeavor, as brilliant, talented, and gifted as you are—*someone out there is better.* Someone has more of what you want.

Freud also posits the theory of *nature vs. nurture. Nature* grants a predetermined genetic range of performance; *nurture* determines where we land on that spectrum. And he's right. Some are naturally better at things than others. Envying a genetic predisposition is a fruitless endeavor. The cards have been dealt. *They cannot be reshuffled.*

Do not judge your self-worth by perception of another's "status."

Counter envy by measuring *real* progress:

1) Daily time—*undisturbed*—committed to your craft.

2) At a pace and intensity where speed does not compromise quality.

The Golden Hour

Tap into that skill in which you find boundless joy and to which you are naturally inclined. Invest one hour—your *Golden Hour*—daily. Reject envy. You do not compare yourself to others. You do not measure progress on results—you measure progress through intensity, focus, and concentration during your *Golden Hour. Results will inevitably follow.*

The rate of progress within your *Golden Hours* will naturally fluctuate; *this you cannot control.* You *can* control committing an hour a day, every day.

A powerful effect results. With daily discipline, the resulting avalanche of growth fuels itself. Your *Golden Hour* will take on a life of its own—becoming a special time to focus on your highest cause; a rich reward blessing you not only in your craft—but in your confidence, outlook, and ambition in all areas of life.

Progress is power.

Put the *Golden Hour* to work. Envy diminishes in the face of disciplined commitment and the growth that follows. Confidence abounds when we set ambitious goals—and adhere to them. Dismiss the Argentine Lake Ducks of the world. They don't matter. You are learning and growing, or you aren't. *That* is how you take measure. Compare yourself to yesterday's you—

And no other.

> *"You will never have a greater or lesser dominion than that over yourself ... the height of a man's success is gauged by his self-mastery; the depth of his failure by his self-abandonment. ... And this law is the expression of eternal justice. He who cannot establish dominion over himself will have no dominion over others."*
>
> —Leonardo da Vinci

Deadpool: Make it Personal

A simple litmus test: If the first *Deadpool* was for you, so is *Deadpool 2*. High expectations are satisfied. For those offended by violence or unaffected by humor, don't bother. For the rest: *See it.*

The *Deadpool* franchise is lauded as a refreshing alternative to the standard format of other Marvel films. And rightfully so—the R rating is well deserved and an appropriate warning for those expecting anything less. As much fun as the premise indicates, *there is a stronger reason* Deadpool *stands out among its Marvel contemporaries.*

Measuring the stakes, a contrast of opposites:

Standard Marvel movie? Saving a city. Saving a planet. Saving the galaxy. Over and over we've seen this tired formula, knowing before the movie starts that our heroes will ultimately succeed.

The potential loss of all humanity is, counterintuitively, *highly* impersonal. When the stakes are everything everywhere, we're numb to the possible consequences.

Enter *Deadpool 2.*

Like its predecessor, this movie resonates far more than standard action films. The reason is simple, and very powerful—instead of universal consequences, *the stakes are highly personal.*

Dwell on this a moment. The bedrock of the first *Deadpool* is revenge and redemption against an antagonist who, though powerful, does not hold the "fate of the universe" in his hands. In *Deadpool 2*, the stakes are the heart and soul of a young mutant driven by revenge. No army of CGI villains— one pitted against another. This makes the story far more relatable—*and far more personal.* The stakes of both films are reflected in our own lives—we've experienced these emotions and fought personal battles as well. We see part of ourselves in the struggles of our protagonist.

The leadership lesson is this.

There is no one-size-fits-all in a modern economy driven by *Influencer Marketing.* This is marketing and relationship building with a highly personal touch; social media and social approval among respected peers and industry influencers. Traditional methods (television, billboards, full-page advertisements, etc.) are bland. *They're boring.* They're impersonal, forgettable; exhausted in their effectiveness. We have quit noticing them, or caring to.

Looking to raise the stakes with your clients and prospects? *Make it personal.* Tailor your initiative to the subsets of your audience—and the individuals within. Meeting in person matters. A handwritten thank you note matters. Connecting with individuals on social media matters. It's the leader with the open-door policy. Each personal touch creates a powerful connection with your organization. Loyalty follows.

Apply this principle to your gift giving. A thoughtful, hand-written letter will have far more meaning to a client or loved one than forty dollars in lavender candles shipped direct from Amazon.

Make it personal. Raise the stakes of your initiative by digging *deeper*—not broader. And do it now. Capture their hearts and minds.

They will stay with you forever.

"Most of my relationships have been like that—with record companies. I've never had a legitimate business relationship with a company. I've always had a personal relationship with someone in the company."

—Ornette Coleman

Hubble & The Nature of Details

April 24, 1990. *Mission STS-31*. The Space shuttle *Discovery* successfully launches the Hubble Telescope into Low Earth Orbit.

The Hubble Telescope: What should have been a crown jewel of flawless preparation and pristine execution for NASA becomes an exercise in futility. A mirror error—*equal to one-fiftieth the thickness of a human hair*—cripples the $1.5 billion telescope. The fix requires eleven months of preparation, a crew of seven astronauts, and a week of labor in space.

After an arduous road to course-correct, success: Hubble has proven a versatile research tool, whose gifts captivate the world. None in astronomy will forget what Hubble has given us. *All will remember the trying times getting there.* Regardless of what Hubble has since accomplished, its legacy will always be interwoven with its failed launch. We must learn, and apply, this cautionary lesson.

The leadership lesson is this.

Sweat the details. Each time. *Every time.*

Invest in doing so without exception. Expend all needed resources to launching with 100% confidence. Anticipate challenges and unforeseen consequences. The price of fixing an error on the back end is *obscenely* disproportionate to initial costs. As is the price of producing an error. Of delivering a flawed product. In money, in time, in credibility, in reputation.

Check. Re-check. *Check again.*

Nail it on the front end—or pay forever on the back end. As the Russian proverb states, *Doveryai, no proveryai.*

Trust, but verify.

> *"The least initial deviation from the truth is multiplied later a thousandfold."*
>
> —Aristotle

The Trial of Elon Musk

1519. Spain. An expedition sails from Seville. Its goal: Circumnavigate the globe. Commanded by Ferdinand Magellan, and after his untimely death, finished by Juan Sebastian Elcano in 1522—the mission is a success. *Man's boundaries greatly expanded. The impossible achieved.*

July 20, 1969. American astronaut Neil Armstrong walks on the moon—a first for humankind. *Man's boundaries greatly expanded. The impossible achieved.*

August, 2012. *Voyager I,* traveling *over 10 miles per second,* becomes the first spacecraft to escape our solar system into the unexplored realm of interstellar space. *Man's boundaries greatly expanded. The impossible achieved.*

Next: Mars colonized. *Man's boundaries will be greatly expanded. The impossible will be achieved.*

~~~

Meet Elon Musk. Born in South Africa, Musk is a technology engineer and entrepreneur with *many* active projects:

SolarCity. *Clean energy panels powering residential and commercial buildings, reducing the cost of traditional roofing through energy savings and longevity. Sustainable and economical.*

Hyperloop One. Proposed by Musk in 2013; under strategic development with Richard Branson's *Virgin Group.* The hyperloop concept: ultra-fast transportation at twice the speed of the world's fastest bullet train (Los Angeles to San Francisco in 35 minutes at 760 mph). Departures anticipated *every thirty seconds.*

The Boring Company. Tunnel construction company transporting vehicles below ground at 130 mph, reducing travel time and relieving congestion on city streets. Potential to eliminate congestion entirely; unlike the limited space of surface roads, tunnels can be dug in multiple layers.

Tesla. Automotive and energy company pioneering electric vehicle transportation. Vehicles with clean, renewable energy and autonomous navigation: A Tesla Model 3, *with no user control,* navigates from Los Angeles, CA to Manhattan, NY in 50 hours, 16 minutes, and 32 seconds *with a $100 cost in total energy.* The owner can share the vehicle with others; a single, autonomous solution managing an entire family's transportation needs. Your car will do the job for you.

SpaceX. Reusable, self-landing rockets achieving dramatic reductions in per-ton space travel and launch-ready turnaround times. Also developing **Starship;** a **massive** reusable rocket so large it can transport the maximum capacity fuel, passengers, and cargo of a Boeing 747—*and the weight of the plane itself*—as its payload.

Musk has other business interests in neurotechnology, artificial intelligence, and potentially, journalism. He also has many detractors.

The critics are many. The concerns are fair.

Critics say his companies expand too fast to remain stable; like so many historical empires, his will overextend, fail to consolidate gains, and ultimately collapse under its own weight. That Musk is eliminating job security through automation. He is *too involved* with his organizations—his micromanagement of each a barrier to their ultimate success. His impact is diluted by being too active on too many projects; spread too thin in too many directions. He is overinvolved in his responses to critics, often tangling himself in public feuds. He has concerning behavior as well: touting the benefits of Ambien and alcohol for sleep (a dangerous combination) on social media, and smoking marijuana during a live interview. Tesla stock dipped *immediately*.

Most egregious of all was a social media post from Musk: "*Am considering taking Tesla private at $420*"—stating funding was secure to do so. This caused an uproar with investors; it was a shocking revelation, and it egregiously misrepresented Tesla's fair market value. It was also a reference to cannabis. The episode ended with a $20 million dollar fine by the SEC.

Musk should have never done it. Once he did, he should have apologized. His brazen response: The fine was "*total bs*" and "*worth it.*"

For the face of a publicly traded company, such actions are perceived as indicators of instability. Shareholders have every right to be concerned; their investment is jeopardized every time Musk oversteps.

Musk's vision:

Change the world for all humanity. Clean power. Sustainable energy. Faster, more affordable transportation. Space travel. And, most boldly of all, a plan to preserve our species through Mars colonization.

Consider this: Colonizing Mars requires renewable energy. Connecting colonies requires ultra-fast travel. Colonization requires underground infrastructure. Clean, cost-efficient transportation is necessary. Leaving Earth—and returning—requires efficient space travel. Transporting people and machinery demands an enormous payload.

Let's look closer.

Colonizing Mars requires renewable energy. *SolarCity*. Connecting colonies requires ultra-fast travel. *Hyperloop*. Colonization requires underground infrastructure. *The Boring Company*. Clean, cost-efficient transportation is necessary. *Tesla*. Leaving Earth—and returning—requires efficient space travel. *SpaceX*. Transporting people and machinery demands an enormous payload. *Starship*.

This is not science fiction. Mars—the next great human achievement—is on the horizon. *Elon Musk is the reason.*

VERDICT.

Change is necessary.

Play the track forward—humanity's non-renewable resource consumption is unsustainable. Musk sees this inevitability. His goal: reduction by degrees of magnitude in the timetable required to save us from ourselves. Much of Musk's technology is open source—a daring challenge to his competitors to do better. The book is open. Do your best. *We'll change the world together.*

The efficiencies of automation will indeed eliminate jobs. New technology always disrupts an established order upon which many livelihoods depend. Modern-day Luddites fight the need for change—and the insecurity it brings. Socioeconomic adjustments will have to unfold. The world Musk envisions is needed. It is necessary.

History will judge Musk as one of our generation's most important figures. The detractors, and their arguments, will fade away. Many visionaries are underappreciated, or misunderstood entirely, in their time. Future generations will herald Musk's work. He will be in the pantheon of history's greats.

Anaximander. Posidonius. Gilberd. Galileo. Cassini. Huygens. Newton. Halley. Messier. Herschel. Leavitt. Einstein. Hubble. Shapley. Drake. Hartmann. Hawking. **Musk**.

We *will* colonize Mars. Elon Musk is the reason.

Consider the full scope of Musk's contributions. Each is grounded in the boldness to think big: In every project he takes on, Musk dares to envision himself at the center of humanity's next giant leap forward. For all his faults, we can confidently state this man has never questioned whether he is capable of transforming the world. Neither should you or I.

Think big. Think bold. Understand that you are capable of being a vision-ary. Let this ignite your untapped potential: *How much more can you and I accomplish?*

In one word: *legacy.*

What will yours be?

> *"The future doesn't belong to the fainthearted; it belongs to the brave."*
>
> —Ronald Reagan

SECTION IV
ME, YOU, AND THEM: BUILDING GREAT TEAMS

Alien: The Art of Empathy

***Alien,* 1979.**

The crew of the *Nostromos,* a deep space cargo vessel, answer a distress signal. Three crew members disembark to investigate while, back on the *Nostromos*, the onboard computer reinterprets the message. It is not a call for help. It is a warning. Our crew stumble upon an alien of unmatched evil. This beast makes sport of terrorizing the *Nostromos* crew. Deaths are inhumane, cruel, brutal; obscene. Human bodies serve as incubators for the young. Human lives—*meaningless.*

With palpable tension, Ripley makes it to the escape pod—*and freedom.* Moments later, we discover the dreaded Xenomorph lurking in her midst. It does not immediately attack her. Outwitting her savage opponent, Ripley releases noxious fumes moments before the monster's anticipated ritualistic bloodletting begins. Ripley jettisons our monster outside the escape pod, activating the engines to slay her deadly foe. Good conquers evil.

The end.

~~~

We now view this story through the eyes of the Xenomorph.

~~~

You burst into the world from the body of your host, oblivious to your surroundings. You react with typical animal behavior: freeze, fight, or flight. *Where am I? What am I? Should I move? Stay? Am I safe? Am I in danger?* You freeze for a moment; confused disorientation. You are in a white room full of beings who stare at you, frozen and transfixed. Driven by the accurate perception of a potential threat, you flee.

Your body begins growing with unprecedented speed—doubling and redoubling within *hours*. The caloric demands of your metabolism force you into immediate action. As a predator, you require prey. There's nothing malicious to this—like all animal species, you are designed to compete for survival. Resources are limited. You use all predatory means available to acquire them. The *only* source of food available? The crew itself. After devouring almost everyone, you have sated your body's needs.

Something is off. This place is noisy. It's restless. The one remaining prey is terrified and moving. Leaving, and quickly. *This must mean something.* Compelled by intuition to flee this unstable environment, you hide in the very place your prey is going. *Safety.*

And there you stay.

The last prey is there, within reach. *But you do not attack.* Having easily defeated others of this species, you do not deem this one a worthy threat. It isn't life or death for you. There's no inherent pleasure in killing. There's no need to kill out of self-defense. You may get hungry later. You may need a host body for reproduction. Until necessary, the prey will remain untouched.

After being detected by this other species, you show no aggression. You have no response. You are willing to survive through cohabitation, demonstrated through your calm demeanor. Your inactivity.

Then, you are viciously attacked. Your survival response: *neutralize the threat, or die.* Now it *is* life or death. You are blown out of the ship. You are tethered to it. You desperately scramble to survive. A searing blast of heat engulfs you, your final experience after just days of conscious awareness.

The end.

~ ~ ~

"Empathy: the action of understanding, being aware of, and vicariously experiencing the feelings, thoughts, and experiences of another."

One story. Two *very* different perspectives. At face value, Alien is a monster movie. A monster who feeds off the thrill of fear, death, and destruction.

It isn't. Revisit *Alien.* All initial assumptions about the Xenomorph are wrong. This is no monster. It has no supernatural abilities. It is an animal, following the same mandates as all animals—adapt, evolve; reproduce. *Survive.* Morality, cruelty, malice, and savagery are not relevant. There is no "evil"—only the desire for life.

Killing humans is no more an ethical conundrum than a lizard eating a cricket, or—once hunger is satisfied—ignoring the cricket entirely.

The leadership lesson is this.

It is easy to misunderstand the *otherness* of others. People operate based on their own needs, frustrations, and desires. *Theirs are rarely the same as yours.* Seek understanding before passing judgement. Empathize. Slow down. *Reassess.*

Right/wrong. Good/evil. Selfish/Altruistic. Reject the impulse of a snap verdict. It is often wrong. You share this world with everyone else—but the lens you experience it through is uniquely yours. *As is theirs.*

Empathy. As important as *what* is *why*.

Understand both before passing judgement.

"We shall listen, not lecture; learn, not threaten. We will enhance our safety by earning the respect of others and showing respect for them. In short, our foreign policy will rest on the traditional American values of restraint and empathy, not on military might."

—Theodore C. Sorensen

Conflict is Crucial: Why TED Talks Suck

In one word: *conflict*. Yes, there are upsides to TED Talks. Adding a "cool factor" to generally boring, monotonous topics does increase awareness of them. Let's agree there's value in learning what one doesn't know, that new perspectives broaden one's horizons, etc.

So few reasons TED Talks *don't* suck—and so many reasons they do. A presentation format that once shattered paradigms has now become stale and formulaic. Eighteen minutes of the same: *personal story, presentation topic, epiphany connecting the two*. One moment, we're riding high. We're soaring with eagles. The next, we're suffering through heart-gripping lows—vicariously feeling the pain the presenter experienced during a troubling, though ultimately enlightening, episode of their lives.

There is a *very* real problem with TED Talks, and it is this: Authentic progress is a byproduct of innovation AND argument. *Highlighted and reemphasized*:

Authentic progress is a byproduct of innovation AND argument.

The most important ingredient in meaningful change: conflict. TED Talks offer an all-you-can-eat buffet of "innovative concepts," all marvels to be praised. By the end of the presentation the room bursts into applause; many in tears, all on their feet, overcome by a collective, mind-blowing orgasm leaving none in the presentation hall untouched. The topic doesn't matter—

it will be met with religious zeal. After all, It's a TED Talk. It must be legitimate.

The fundamental error here: Innovation is only half—*and the lesser half*—of meaningful progress. Reckless, unchecked progress is dangerous. Scientific, social, and technological advances *demand* representation from proponents and detractors alike. An intelligent, educated decision requires a holistic approach: Truly enlightened people seek the arguments both for and against anything.

We need peer-reviewed studies. We need counter-punches to brilliant, form-breaking concepts. We need the downside *more* than the upside. Let us judge for ourselves.

Unchecked social progress is, quite literally, deadly. The most dangerous regimes in history became so under the mantle of "social progress," with dissidents stifled—or eliminated entirely. Is this an extreme example? Tragically, no. Look to the past. How many revolutions started with positive intentions only to descend into slaughter and genocide?

There MUST be voices representing each perspective.

TED Talks captivate with emotional fervor not through the truth of their ideas, but the passion of the presenter and the format of the presentation itself. Caught up in the emotional energy of the moment, dogmatic, unquestioning empathy voids truth and logic.

> *"TED: a monstrosity that turns scientists and thinkers into low-level entertainers, like circus performers."*
>
> —Nassim Nicholas Taleb,
> globally acclaimed
> statistician and author

The leadership lesson is this.

ARGUE *EVERYTHING*.

Groupthink is infectious. A room of decision makers often gravitate around the opinions of the leader, unconsciously aware of their conformity to the leader's ideals. Self-preservation through favor compels this.

A presenter should present not only their innovative concept, but its pitfalls, challenges, and potential repercussions as well. As a presenter, you are responsible to give the entire story of your concept—the good and the bad alike. It is on the group to ask meaningful questions and challenge new concepts *in every way they can*. A vetted strategy doesn't guarantee success, but it does ensure a greater chance for success by identifying—and planning for—unforeseen challenges and unintended consequences.

This is impossible for one person to do alone. Unconscious self-bias will trump objectivity. Unlike TED Talks, which captivate audiences by appealing to emotion, your job is to address your topic with unemotional distance—attending to the bad no less than the good. All of it. The hardest part of this: removing one's ego from the equation. Being a catalyst for positive change is a force within each of us. That same force, however, blinds us to the downside of our initiatives. It isn't easy to invest oneself in a project willfully critiqued by qualified colleagues.

Leaders: You *must* create an environment acknowledging the need for conflict, acknowledging conflict creates the strongest outcome, and that it is on us—*all of us*—to be skeptics of new ideas regardless of their source. Let the room know we are not attacking the person; not their effort, commitment, or engagement—but challenging their ideas only. Set this expectation at the beginning of every meeting. Demonstrate this by having employees argue for and against all concepts—it is a universal rule applying to everyone, including leadership. *Including you.*

Demonstrate to your team that *skepticism* is a core value of your culture. It is a pillar of your organization. That *all* ideas are challenged.

Again: Authentic progress is a byproduct of innovation *AND* argument. Meaningful change *demands* conflict.

That conflict begins with you.

"Blind belief in authority is the greatest enemy of truth."

—Albert Einstein

The Shape of Water: On Fundamental Needs

In a classified research facility, a janitor discovers a connection with a unique creature being held against its will. *This film is stunning in its execution.* The perfectly executed Cold War backdrop. The gothic, visual tribute to Old Hollywood. The acting, casting, directing, sweeping musical score; all masterfully executed in service to the story—*and what a story it is.* Gift wrapped and delivered in the iconic, signature style exclusively Guillermo del Toro's.

Four Oscars, including Best Picture. The story itself: a powerful metaphor for the fundamental human needs universal to all of us. Del Toro—through the unique connection between our two protagonists—offers not only a bold statement against prejudice, but also a challenge to search for prejudice within ourselves.

Richard Strickland, our antagonist, embodies countless prejudices. While the broad scope of these prejudices being assigned to one actor could verge on caricature, actor Michael Shannon brilliantly portrays the very worst of humanity. His is an effective, believable, authentic performance; *judge this by your growing detestation of him—and the values he embodies—as the movie progresses.*

The best stories leave us contemplating their message—reflecting on the experience long after the curtain is drawn. It is possible *The Shape of Water* is unmatched in doing so among its modern contemporaries—its powerful themes of universal human needs, of detesting prejudice in every form, and the transcendence of what connects us over the triviality of what divides us—deeply resonate.

The need for safety. Connection. Respect. Love. These are the drivers motivating every character in *The Shape of Water*, shaping their actions for good or for evil. These are the needs that spur our protagonists to overpower the forces that seek to keep them apart.

These fundamental truths affect every life. They extend to your organization as well. We will explore them through *Maslow's Hierarchy of Needs*, a map of human behavioral motivation developed by renowned psychologist Abraham Maslow (*Maslow's Hierarchy of Needs; "A Theory of Human Motivation"*—Psychological Review, *1943.*). Each need must be met before ascending to the next; we start at base level and work up.

#5: Physiological.

In life:

Food, warmth, rest, shelter.

In your organization:

Basic necessities. Break room, well ventilated air, clean facilities, proper lighting, access to food and drink. *If you're somehow getting this wrong, punch yourself in the face—or let your team do it for you.* They'll want to—and you'll deserve it. Open up the company coffers. Soda, coffee, tea, etc. This minimal gesture has excellent impact on morale.

#4: Safety.

In life:

Law, order, protection, security.

In your organization:

A non-hostile work environment is mandatory. A safe, secure workplace. Leaders, this one is critical to you: Team members first filter trust in the organization through the lens of *you*. A trustworthy, empathetic leader is the most important resource for every employee. *If you, dear leader, are not a champion for your team, you are not leading.*

#3: Love/belonging.

In life:

Friendship, intimacy, affection, acceptance.

In your organization:

Unite your team; fuel cohesion. Commit to group recreational time *during* traditional work hours—this shows you mean it. Schedule time for fun. Create learning and leadership opportunities. Brainstorming, mentoring, team building, activities at work; *optional* activities outside of work—each interpersonal connection between team members strengthens your organization. The stronger the team, the more impactful the results.

#2: Esteem.

In life:

Independence, achievement, status, self-confidence.

In your organization:

Recognition and rewards. Modest, high-frequency recognition is much more valuable than a once-a-year epic splash. Weekly recognition of peak performers keeps morale up. Making recognition a habit doesn't just increase culture—*it adds a new pillar of strength to your organization*. Top-performing organizations constantly celebrate success.

#1: Self-actualization.

In life:

Self-fulfillment; peak performance. Realization of one's full potential.

In your organization:

This is the level colleagues reach when all prior needs are satisfied. This is the ultimate goal. These are your rock stars; the very best. Engage them fully. They are given leadership roles. They are given opportunities to advance. They are given raises without asking. They function as mentors. They model organizational values and see their work not as a job—*but as a cause.*

~~~

Maslow's Hierarchy of Needs offers a roadmap for increasing employee engagement, regardless the nature of your organization. Contextualize each step with your leadership group—what are we getting right? Where can we improve? How can we get better?

Put the steps to action. They will fuel growth. They will fuel engagement. They will fuel culture. They will get results. A unified team of self-actualized contributors can do far more than change the world—*they can build a new one.* This is your goal.

You now know the steps. Take them.

"I would say that an understanding of man's intrinsic needs, and of the necessity to search for a climate in which those needs could be realized, is fundamental to the education of the designer."

—Paul Rand

On War: The Art of Persuasion

"War is the continuation of politics by other means."

—Carl von Clausewitz

Interpretation: We use force to impose our will. *We use force to get what we want.* What if there's a better way? What if we temper the heavy hand of authority through the art of persuasion?

Meet Carl Philipp Gottfried von Clausewitz. A Prussian military general and theorist, von Clausewitz's pioneering work, *On War* (a 9,000-page German tome) remains a seminal text in the study of modern warfare. Credentials:

A soldier at age twelve. Campaign in France—1792-1793. Attended Berlin General War School. Captured by the French during the Jena Campaign; 1806. Russian and German campaigns—1812-1813. Pivotal role in the Convention of Tauroggen, uniting Prussia, Russia, and the United Kingdom in victory against France at Waterloo, 1815. Director of the Kriegsakademie, the highest military college in the Kingdom of Prussia. Rejoins the Army in 1830; appointed Chief of Staff during the Polish Insurrection of 1830-1831.

Credentials now established, *forget about them*. Let's look to the lesson.

The Clausewitzian Trinity

A loose interpretation, and one of many of **On War**, *The Trinity* posits three elements to effective warfare:

1) People

2) Army

3) Government

The superior strategist designs his or her campaign to appeal to each, building support at all levels through uniquely crafted means. Organizational change requires buy-in from all stakeholders. *The Trinity* is the answer. In von Clausewitz's sophisticated magnum opus we find a practical, powerful strategy for getting things done.

The modern agent of change, and the effective persuader, understand this: *Change must appeal to all parties involved—and customized to each accordingly.* The change must entice the stakeholder's self-interest; there is no shortcut, there is no blanket solution, there is only understanding the specific goals of all involved and the unique circumstances of each. Burdening others with *what they owe you* is the fastest way to changing nothing. Nobody cares what you think you're owed. You must show how your initiative, though it may be challenging in the short-term, ultimately brightens *their* future. There is no tool of influence stronger than universal appeal.

Application.

Teacher:

We propose a new policy affecting the school. We must appeal to the people, the army, and the government.

People: *students.*

Army: *fellow teachers.*

Government: *senior staff, educational board, directors.*

We tailor the benefits of our proposal to each. *What do they stand gain?*

~~~

Coach:

We propose additional practice time to strengthen the team. We must appeal to the people, the army, and the government.

People: *Players.*

Army: *Parents.*

Government: *Fellow coaches.*

We tailor the benefits of our proposal to each. *How does this serve their self-interest?*

~~~

Leader:

We propose a sweeping reform affecting all levels of the organization. We must appeal to the people, the army, and the government.

People: *workforce.*

Army: *management.*

Government: *owners, executives; board of directors.*

We tailor the benefits of our proposal to each. *How do the cost, time, and effort of your initiative appeal at all levels?*

~~~

"Because leadership says so," "Because they should want to," "They'll deal with it," "They'll have to manage"—none of these are the tools of effective leaders. They may work in the short-term, but ultimately unravel. Blanket, organizational-wide mandates are the blunt weapons of a dictator, with repercussions ultimately working against not only the proposed change itself,

but also those proposing it. Do not do this. *The Trinity* transforms change from obligation to appeal.

You are an agent of change; a champion of influence. You strategize. You deeply consider all involved. You appeal to the self-interest of each. You build an action plan using *The Trinity*, executing the process with a strategic mindset and focused discipline. Meaningful progress ensues. Put Clausewitz's *Trinity* to work; there is no strategy more powerful for inciting change. You are now a modern-day military strategist.

You are now a master of the art of persuasion.

"Strategy is a commodity, execution is an art."

—Peter F. Drucker

Inception: Substance over Style

Christopher Nolan's filmography: when an industry's best collaborate in a singular glorious enterprise. Innovation without precedent, redefining the craft's high water mark. Each film an engaging and immersive experience.

Except for *Inception*.

Understand how the filmmaker works. It is not by finding interesting ideas—it's finding those worthy of feature-length treatment. Recall the theatrics of *Inception*: Gravity-free action. *A freight train plows down a crowded city street. A decrepit metropolis slides into the ocean like a dying glacier. A suburban landscape folds over itself.* All novel ideas, none of which stand alone on their own merit. None that can sustain a feature-length narrative.

Stanley Kubrick (unlike Nolan) starts with a cohesive story and layers in groundbreaking scenes. Nolan (unlike Kubrick) grabs duct tape and pours his leftovers all over the kitchen table. How to bind this narrative mess together? Simple: dreams. Done.

Nolan is cheating here. Visualize *Inception* with another director. Without Michael Caine and Leonardo DiCaprio, who can carry any story; even one this abhorrent. The best table scraps from the best filmmaker do not combine to make a meal. We are left with all style, and—ultimately—no substance. This results in a film so confusing that three quarters of its run length are spent in exposition explaining what you'll see in the final act, which begins long after the viewer quits trying (or cares) to understand the disaster unfolding before them.

This is a bad movie. This is bad storytelling, poorly told. While visually appealing, there's no unifying structure combining the elements of this tedious, plodding abomination. No grand strategy. Remove the film's contributors and look at the story itself—a pointless, failed concept resulting in a pointless, failed film.

The leadership lesson is this.

Grand strategy:

"A comprehensive, long-term plan of essential actions by which a firm plans to achieve its major objectives. Key factors of this strategy may include market, product, and/or organizational development through acquisitions, divestiture, diversification, joint ventures, or strategic alliances."

1) Start with a master vision.

2) Then work backwards, identifying necessary *essential actions.*

3) These actions form your Grand Strategy.

You cannot combine favorite—even effective—*essential actions* and *"see how it goes."* You will not stumble into brilliance. You will never achieve an undefined goal. *Essential actions* form the spine of your ultimate goal. This basic exercise gives you the breadth of what lies ahead. This is the proverbial 30,000 foot view. Once *essential actions* are identified, set to work assigning roles and responsibilities. With a broad scope of what's needed, *now* you build the depth chart.

Begin at the end. Then—and *only* then—build the blueprint to get there.

> *"All men can see these tactics whereby I conquer, but what none can see is the strategy out of which victory is evolved."*
>
> —Sun Tzu

The Art of Simplicity

In Art.

14th century. The Pope, commissioning a painter for a significant project, sends a courier to art's grandest stage: Florence, Italy. The courier collects submissions in the style of the day: overwhelming grandeur; excessive opulence. Artist Giotto di Bondone submits a masterpiece: a bright red circle— *a perfect circle*—executed in a single stroke. Elegant, accurate; *powerful*. Giotto tells the courier the Pope will understand the implication of such precision. Giotto is right. He wins the commission.

In Cinema.

Five famous lines. Say each out loud, then state the movie.

"*Show me the money.*"

"*I'll be back.*"

"*Go ahead, make my day.*"

"*You talkin' to me?*"

"*You can't handle the truth.*"

Not only do we recall the quotes themselves, we remember the source—and the rhythm and cadence of each. The critical commonality: Not *one* of these enduring quotes *is over five words long.*

In literature.

A timeless comparison: *classics vs. moderns.* The modern novel averages 100,000-175,000 words in length. Three classics and their word count:

Margaret Mitchell's **Gone with the Wind**: 418,053.

Leo Tolstoy's **War and Peace**: 587,287.

Victor Hugo's **Les Misérables**: 655,478.

The lesson is simple: in context of our modern world, *less is far more.*

Simplicity wins.

Modern art, in all its forms, competes for the very limited attention of a relentlessly preoccupied society. To a degree unseen in human history, we're barraged from every direction with sensory overload. Undivided time and attention have never been so scarce a resource.

Context is necessary to understand why. In the days of the classics, a novel got one through a long winter indoors, where time and attention competed *with nothing.* A long novel, and the elegant prose of the day, were treasures to be discovered—the length of the book a virtue, not a vice. How times have changed. Current novels are not only shorter—the prose itself is tighter, crisper; easier to digest. Literature once filling countless free hours now competes for the limited attention of a distracted daily commute.

Google is the most popular internet search engine. Its minimalist platform has universal appeal; we are invited in by its elegant simplicity. Open a browser to Google, and a second to Yahoo! Compare the two. Yahoo!

delivers a barrage of information; no page space goes unfilled. Simplicity wins. Google's *less* is far more.

Application.

The effective leader does not use the biggest words in the longest phrases. Ideas are communicated in plain language with brevity. The most important component of writing is *editing*. Not what is said—*but what isn't.*

Be your own editor.

Cut *everything* down to its core constituents. Stop over-communicating. Reduce the overblown presentation slides down to single sentences; singles words; better yet—*single images.* This will ignite audience engagement.

The longer the email, the more likely we are to delete it. *Get to the point.*

Anyone can ramble on about their subject for 45 minutes. Impress me. Sift your message down with such granularity it can be relayed in 8 to 12 minutes: a realistic time frame to educate—and entice—your audience.

Remove bloated "resume speak" from your vocabulary; while you're impressed with your fancy words, your audience is wondering what the hell you're talking about. Be yourself. Just talk to them.

Less is more. Brevity is power. Simplicity wins. Get to the point.

They will love you for it.

> *"Knowledge is a process of piling up facts; wisdom lies in their simplification."*
> —Martin H. Fischer

SECTION V
LIVING YOUR PRINCIPLES

There Will Be Blood:
Lawsuits & The Faustian Bargain

Table seven.

You glance at your cards; pocket Aces. You check, noting the player in position three is eager to bet—and predictably does so. Appropriately, you re-raise for the ultimate stakes: all-in. Without hesitation, Player Three calls. **Massive pot.** The room watches.

Confidently, your opponent reveals their hand. Unsuited **7** and **10.**

All-in on a 7 and a 10. *A statistical long shot. A disastrous call.*

Your aces stand strong.

Flop: 9 J K

Excellent flop—your pocket aces lead.

Turn: A

Triplets. Now on the board: **9 J K A.**

River: 8

8 9 J K A.

Inside straight on the River. **All in on a 7 and a 10.**

The bad beat. Your Aces defeated by a straight. An oblivious call from a clueless player making a horrible play. And rewarded for it; his answer: "*I felt lucky.*"

The dealer rakes the pot.

~~~

Rake: the scaled fee taken by a cardroom; generally, 2.5% to 10% of each pot.

~~~

And so, you commit to doling out divine justice. You buy back in with a simple goal in mind: **vengeance.** The game continues.

The dealer rakes the pot.

Mostly highs; some lows. You're building a strong stack. Mr. Lucky is whittling away.

The dealer rakes the pot.

Players come. Players go. The hours go by.

The dealer rakes the pot.

Ultimately, **success.**

Mr. Lucky glances at his chip stack: just a few dollars. Down many hundreds. You smile—he's busted. Your faith in The Divine restored.

Until looking at your stack. It, too, is an echo of what it was. The dealer sits back and smiles, acknowledging what you and Mr. Lucky didn't: With every pot rake, both chip stacks are drained away. It was an inevitable outcome; with enough time—with a consistent rake—the House always wins.

Your goal is accomplished: **Mr. Lucky lost.**

But you did not win.

~~~

Faust; Faustian:

"A situation in which an ambitious person surrenders moral integrity in order to achieve power and success."

So the German legend goes: Faust sells his soul to the devil to *"win."* To feed the ego, pride, and arrogance which must be sated.

~~~

There Will be Blood

Daniel Plainview: **ruthless.**

Though himself without faith, Daniel succumbs to the pressure of Eli Sunday, a young minister demanding a charitable donation to divinely "bless" Daniel's new oil well and procure the town's favor. Over the course of the story, Daniel's animosity turns to hatred. Once an inconvenience to deal with—Eli has become a bitter rival; a symbol of all Daniel despises.

The film ends with the humiliation of Eli. Daniel dismantles Eli's faith before beating him to death:

> *"It was (your brother) Paul who was chosen ... he's the prophet. He's the smart one ... they should have put you in a glass jar on the mantelpiece."*

At all costs, Daniel would defeat his bitter rival. *Yet, he does not win.* He is not victorious. In defeating his rival Daniel has damned himself. He has sold his soul. As Daniel notes in the film's final line:

"I'm finished."

~~~

Ego, Arrogance, and Lawsuits

Over 2% of the US GDP goes to tort costs—the highest in any industrialized nation. We are immersed in a litigious society.

Make no mistake: A lawsuit doesn't have to go in your opponent's favor to take a crippling toll on you. Regardless of the outcome, the process itself will deplete you. It will loom over your work. It will be an unspoken guest at your dinner table. It will consume your life, your money, your health; your outlook, your demeanor; your wellbeing. And ultimately, who is the biggest winner?

The law firm. The lawyer. The rake. The pot. *The card dealer.*

As time goes on, legal fees will feed at the trough of you and your opponent's resources. They will incessantly rake the pot. Exhausted and destitute, nothing will remain.

The leadership lesson is this.

Be ***painfully aware*** of the premises fueling litigation. Be ***wholly certain*** of the motive behind your legal action—is it pride? The need to win? To flex a willpower stronger than your opponents'? Are you needlessly pushing for more at the mutual cost of both parties? *Have you removed your ego from the outcome?*

Daniel Plainview defeated his enemy—*and ultimately lost*. Faust got the power he craved—*and ultimately lost*.

Let theirs be a vicarious lesson.

> *"For what shall it profit a man, if he shall gain the whole world, and lose his own soul?"*
>
> Mark 8:36, King James Version

Nelson Mandela: The Art of Negotiation

Nelson Mandela.

South Africa's first President elected through true representative democracy. An icon of social justice, unwavering principles, and the power of unity through reconciliation. He is the recipient of over 250 honors, including the Nobel Peace Prize.

Revolutionary. Political leader. Philanthropist. President. ***Prisoner.***

~~~

Working as a lawyer, Mandela commits himself to African national politics. He is the voice of opposition to the white-only government established by *apartheid*, a racially segregated political system. Mandela is unyielding in his defiance of the oppressive apartheid government. In 1962, he is arrested for conspiracy to overthrow the state. The sentence: prison for life.

His incarceration begins.

~~~

Mandela is offered release multiple times over the course of his imprisonment. The terms are simple: *Denounce your political beliefs. Stop your advocacy. You will live out a simple, quiet life. Agree to these terms, and you are released.*

Mandela reflects on the proposal. *Their terms* are not a release into freedom—only further bondage. A subjugation designed to neutralize the impact of his purpose.

Mandela's bold response: *"Only free men can negotiate."* He will die in prison for his principles before abandoning them to an artificial *"freedom."*

<center>~~~</center>

27 years later; 1990.

The pressure to free Mandela is tremendous. Fearing racial civil war, President F. W. de Klerk releases him. *27 years in prison*. The sentence is now over. President de Klerk and Mandela negotiate an end to apartheid.

A multi-racial election follows in 1994. *Mandela is elected President.*

Few historical figures have been such powerful agents of change. Mandela, through his negotiating strategy, changed the world. Let's explore his strategy, looking at Mandela's inner and outer approach.

Inner approach:

"As I walked out the door toward the gate that would lead to my freedom, I knew if I didn't leave my bitterness and hatred behind, I'd still be in prison."

How natural to seek revenge, justice, and punitive measures against his captors. *With relentless courage*, Mandela abandons these impulses entirely. His path forward, in his own words, would be that of *goodness* and *forgiveness*. The task ahead will not accommodate deeply harbored feelings of resentment.

For Mandela, the outward change he seeks starts within: Abandon animosity. Walk in forgiveness, and compassion, and camaraderie.

We now examine Mandela's outer approach.

"A good leader can engage in a debate frankly and thoroughly, knowing that at the end he and the other side must be closer, and thus emerge stronger. You don't have that idea when you are arrogant, superficial, and uninformed."

Mandela's belief: Meet with your opposition. Not from a position of power, authority, and your version of justice—but from a position of shared humanity and higher purpose.

"No one is born hating another person because of the color of his skin, or his background, or his religion. People must learn to hate, and if they can learn to hate, they can be taught to love, for love comes more naturally to the human heart than its opposite."

—*Nelson Mandela*

True agents of influence share this belief:

Outward progress begins within.

It does not begin with "*them*."

It begins with you, and I—**here**, and *now*.

We set aside animosity. We abandon the base desires of revenge, and punishment, and justice.

World changers know:

The best in us brings out the best in others.

We do not compromise our values. We do not compromise core beliefs. We do listen with open hearts and minds to the opposition, seeking solutions that benefit both parties.

It's a mindset shift from **us vs. them** to ...

US.

~~~

Negotiation Tactics

1) Define your lowest acceptable range BEFORE entering negotiations. This removes getting caught up in the fever and allowing

too many concessions. Before starting, you've internally established your bottom line. Do not waver.

2) *Ask for more.* Negotiating down allows the other side to feel you are making concessions based on their influence. Allow this. Ask for more up front, then *appear* to meet in the middle—which in truth of fact is the outcome originally desired.

3) Look for creative win/win solutions. Can a low-cost concession in one area add value to the other side? Service on top of the sale? What other factors can we consider? Work together for mutually beneficial solutions.

4) This point is the most important: **Be willing to walk away.** Yes, you care; yes, you want to find agreeable terms. But ultimately, you are very willing to walk. Take a step back—*and watch them take two steps forward.*

~~~

In Mandela's own words:

"If you want to make peace with your enemy, you have to work with your enemy. Then he becomes your partner."

Nelson Mandela has done his part to build Heaven on Earth. He has shown us the road.

Let us now take it.

"Let us never negotiate out of fear. But let us never fear to negotiate."
—John F. Kennedy

Avatar: Work the Plan

Avatar. A masterpiece of planning. Initially slated for a 1999 release, Avatar went on indefinite hold. The challenge: The available technology was insufficient to execute director James Cameron's vision. The film would be done right—*or not at all.*

Fortunately for us, technology caught up. Cameron delivered an instant classic.

Blockbuster success yields sequels. With strong franchise potential, studios cash in quickly. But not with *Avatar.* Why? More important than technology: story. Four *Avatar* sequels are in production. Four scripts produced together, unified by a grand story arc **only possible through master planning**. Every plant. Every animal. Every syllable of the *Na'vi* thousand-plus word lexicon. What should we expect from the sequels? The history of cinema predicts success. *Let's explore.*

~~~

Three blockbuster franchises:

1) *Jurassic Park*

2) *Alien*

3) *Pirates of the Caribbean*

Each a smash success, promising great things to come.

Now, a sequel for each:

    1) *Jurassic Park III*

    2) *Alien III*

    3) *Pirates of the Caribbean: Dead Man's Chest*

From amazing first films to total disasters. All three follow-ups the least of their counterparts; all three unforgivably bad.

How did this happen?

Jurassic Park III. Alien III. Dead Man's Chest.

In all three movies, *filming began **before** scripts were complete.*

Studios cashed in. Speed over quality. Dialogue and story arcs developed in real time. Poor planning yielded poor results; "*winging it*" going predictably wrong.

History's verdict: Have high expectations for *Avatar's* sequels—with such meticulous planning, they will be extraordinary.

The leadership lesson is this.

PLAN THE WORK.

All of it.

Then,

WORK THE PLAN.

Your brilliant concepts and sterling initiatives mean *nothing* without a defined beginning—*and a defined end*. Whatever time this process takes—**take it**. There is no *"winging it"* for the true leader. There is only careful, cautious planning of every step of the journey.

The *Na'vi's* lesson to us: Before releasing the arrow,

Aim first.

> *"It takes as much energy to wish as it does to plan."*
>
> —Eleanor Roosevelt,
> Former First Lady
> of the United States

Winston Churchill & Public Speaking: Find Your Voice

"Of all the talents bestowed upon men, none is so precious as the gift of oratory. He who enjoys it wields a power more durable than that of a great king. He is an independent force in the world."

—Winston Churchill

Politician. Writer. Army Officer. Prime Minster of the United Kingdom. First Lord of the Admiralty. Winston Churchill's bold, daring leadership— and mastery of oratory—led Britain to victory in World War II.

Churchill will live forever as one of history's greatest orators. Through the power and purpose of his words he galvanized a nation—*and a world*— against fascism and tyranny.

The key to Churchill's public speaking: *Preparation.* Churchill wrote, memorized, and practiced *every* word. In doing so, delivering the speech became the easiest part of his presentation. So immersed in his material, the presentation flowed naturally. *It did not start that way.*

~~~

At the age of 29, a young Churchill speaks to the House of Commons. Once into his speech, Churchill's mind wanders. He loses his focus, stumbling for words that will not come. Minutes roll by. Heckled by the House, Churchill sits down—head in hands—humiliated, defeated.

Churchill was unprepared. *It would be the last time.*

From then on, Churchill immersed himself in his speeches word for word, relentlessly committing them to memory. Churchill learned the lesson: There is no speaker who can "improvise" an impactful presentation. *Not one.* It is not possible.

~~~

Find your Voice.

The single greatest professional skill is finding your voice in front of others. Find comfort in knowing no one is simply "*born with it.*" Those who appear to "just have it" have put in endless effort. It only appears seamless because the real work—***the relentless preparation***—was done well in advance. The presentation is an afterthought of the preparation process.

The power of Churchill's voice is within you—eagerly awaiting discovery. He changed the world through oratory. **So can you.**

Here's how.

~~~

PX3: our presentation roadmap. We're going to nail it.

Our three P's:

Prepare.

Practice.

Present.

~~~

PREPARE. *Practice. Present.*

Story.

We start with story—the ultimate tactic to hook an audience. **Make it something unique to you**. *A hobby, a passion, a talent—you choose. Make it yours. The most powerful stories come from personal experience. Your story leads into the* **body** *of your presentation; a bridge to what follows.*

Body.

We do the heavy lifting here. If we're discussing three major points of our topic, we structure the most influential point for last. We end with impact.

We focus on brevity and economy of words. Use the fewest words, and simplest words, necessary to make your point. We want to pack punch. When presenting, less is far more.

Call to Action.

What good is your discussion if it does not incite change? If it does not create curiosity, or compel action? **Always end with a call to action**. *How your audience can learn more, can contribute to a cause, can follow up with you directly—give them a tangible next step. Without a call to action, you are not an influencer. You are not an agent of change. You are merely an entertainer.*

~~~

Prepare. **PRACTICE.** *Present.*

Practice.

It's life or death for your presentation. Prepare; it's life. "Wing it"—it's death. We are practicing our full presentation, spoken out loud, **three times a day** *for* **three days** *before game day. We stand and speak confidently, a mirror as our audience. We gauge our body language; no crossed arms. Facing forward. Head held high. We listen for verbal "ahhh's" and "uhhmmm's", removing these unnecessary "fillers" from our vocabulary.*

Presentation day. **One final practice.** *We wake up, going through our final recital, and realize it's flowing naturally at this point. Our preparation has paid off. We've got this. The pre-game is now over. It's time to roll.*

~~~

Prepare. Practice. **PRESENT.**

Confident presenters do not run a verbal 40-yard dash. They are calm, cool, collected; in control of their stage presence and themselves.

We're going to slow down. At the same time, we're going to boost our confidence.

There is a moment when it **feels** *like it's time to start.* **We aren't going to.** *A brief pause builds positive tension. It shows you are comfortable. It shows you are confident. The room quiets. The audience leans in. They are now yours.*

When we think it's time to start, we **PAUSE.**

Our three-second inner monologue:

Own the moment. Own the moment. Own the moment.

Now *we start.*

We slow down. *We. Slow. Down.*

WE SPEAK UP.

We keep a calm, controlled pace, speaking with confidence and clarity.

~~~

"To each there comes in their lifetime a special moment when they are figuratively tapped on the shoulder and offered the chance to do a very special thing, unique to them and fitted to their talents. What a tragedy if that moment finds them unprepared or unqualified for that which could have been their finest hour."

—Winston Churchill

~~~

The greatest leaders have one thing in common—none were born great speakers, and all worked *very* hard to earn it. **As it worked for them, so it will work for you.**

We've gone through some basic strategies above. I encourage this process as a first step on a journey that never ends.

Parents: encourage your children to join debate teams. Acting classes. Vocal lessons. They don't have to be politicians, actresses, or singers for these to give them confidence in finding their voices. It's a gift that will bless them their entire lives. And the same goes for you. *Join them.* You'll learn and grow together.

Confidence is a skill gained through focused practice and preparation. You earn it.

The good news: Implementing the **PX3** presentation strategy above will immediately put you in the top 20% of speakers. Most leaders simply don't know the tactics to do it, or understand that, like anything else, it is a skill no one is born with. It must be learned, and it **can** be learned by **anyone**.

Going from the top 20% to the top 5% of speakers will take an enormous investment of time, practice, and diligence.

You can—and should—do it.

Speaking is just one step in a long journey toward launching a successful project or making a positive change. There is much to do. Others will need to share their views, and you will need to discuss every potential benefit and drawback to your vision—and not just the elements of it that sound great in a speech. Your call to action must also be a call to dialogue. Presentation is just one step in a long path to success—*but as the first step, it is the most important.*

It is imperative that you invest in getting it right.

Buy three books on public speaking. I'm less concerned with you getting the one "right book" than making a habit of studying the skill. Each book has something to teach you. All reinforce the craft's underlying core principles.

Presenters in the top 2% are elite. They are also, like Winston Churchill himself, empowered to change the world through mastery of this critical skill. *And you have the ability to join them.*

Find your voice. It will change your life.

It will change your world.

> *"Do not say a little in many words but a great deal in a few."*
> —Pythagoras

No Country for Old Men: The Nature of Change

"What's the most you've ever lost on a coin toss?"

Meet Anton Chigurh: one of Cinema's greatest villains. *Javier Bardem* delivers a profound, complex, and chilling performance. Ours is a villain who—quite literally—views human life as no more significant than cattle. He is essentially unstoppable, knowing what he is doing, where he is going, and how circumstances will transpire. He is a monster, somehow operating on what he believes is a code of ethics. It is early in the film when the viewer realizes there is a *very* real chance Anton will not be stopped.

No Country for Old Men's core message is often misunderstood by the casual viewer. A deeper viewing peels back the layers.

Change.

Change—and *the inevitability of change*—are the primary themes of this movie. The story starts as a classic Western, cloaked in every trope of the genre. Hero. Villain. Good. Evil. Justice. Revenge. High stakes. All of it. This formula is shattered after the midpoint of the film when our protagonist, Llewelyn Moss, is suddenly—and shockingly—found dead.

In a classic Western the hero's showdown with the villain is at the end, we witness the battle, and the hero wins—none of which occur here. Our hero is dead at the end of act two with an entire act of story remaining. There is no showdown with the villain—protagonist Llewelyn is killed offscreen not by the villain, but by peripheral characters. We, alongside Sheriff Ed Tom Bell (Tommy Lee Jones), arrive in the aftermath. Our hero isn't merely defeated—*he was never close to winning.*

No Country for Old Men shatters traditional paradigms, subverting our expectations of heroes and villains, showdowns and resolutions. Every genre trope of the Western story is set up. *Every genre trope of the Western story is broken.*

The thesis of the film: **Change is inevitable**. Circumstances evolve.

The traditional Western story once felt relevant to its audiences. That mold no longer applies to the world we live in today. And the new mold, seen in the world of *No Country for Old Men*, is ugly, harsh, evil; unfathomable. Human nature, void of humanity.

No Country for Old Men is a Western adapted for the times we live in. It reveals a new truth.

~~~

The nature of change is this: With or without you, it will march forward. It will never cease. And the rate of change is greatly accelerating.

Change offers both a challenge and an opportunity.

The challenge—those disconnected from the times will be left behind immediately and entirely.

The opportunity—*boundless* for those incessantly scanning the horizon, constantly course-correcting; relentlessly identifying the opportunities that change *always* creates.

~~~

The ending scene is understood in context once the theme of inevitable change is established. Sheriff Ed Tom Bell, explaining to his wife why he is retiring from law enforcement, speaks of the rich tradition of classic lawmen in earlier times. Working in a world so rational, stable, and predict-able some sheriffs didn't even carry guns.

Sheriff Ed recognizes the world is no longer one of logic and order. He understands he can make no sense of it. Feeling outmatched and ineffec-tive, he retires. His despair is conveyed when describing a dream: It is of his father, going ahead of him, blazing a path through challenging—though familiar—territory. To an established place of comfort and familiarity; a rugged trail carved by the lawmen before him.

That path exists no more. Times have changed. Times will *always* change.

Far faster now than they ever have in the scope of human history.

The paths of *then* are forgotten.

The old molds are left behind. The old molds are broken. You must adapt. You must evolve.

Or you will be left behind with them.

> *"Change is inevitable. Change is constant."*
>   —Benjamin Disraeli

Honoring Our Veterans

Every Memorial Day, the American flag is raised full staff for a moment, then lowered to half. At noon the flag is raised fully once again. The half-staff position honors the brave souls lost in military service. The midday raising by we the living reaffirms our commitment to the principles for which they gave their lives.

How trivial our daily problems and challenges are by comparison.

Never forget the sacrifices that those around you have made for your organization and your community. You built your career from square one, and you should be proud. You also had the opportunity to do so because of others who have sacrificed to create a country and a world where you can thrive. It is only when we recognize the role others have played in our success that we become truly self-aware.

Thank our Veterans. Thank our Service Members. These heroes are all around us—adorned in caps and clothing honoring their service. *Speak with them.*

It is this simple ... ***Thank you. Thank you for your service. Thank you for your sacrifice.***

Model this for your children; have them do the same. Let them meet the Heroes who stand for each of us; for all of us.

Their sacrifice lives forever if we never forget.

> _"Honor to the soldiers and sailors everywhere, who bravely bear their country's cause. Honor, also, to the citizen who cares for his brother in the field and serves, as he best can, the same cause."_
>
> —Abraham Lincoln

Pax Romana: Culture's Reward

Pax Romana. *The Roman Peace.* 27 BC-180 AD. 206 years spanning from the ascension of Ceasar Augustus, Rome's first emperor, to the fall of Marcus Aurelius; *the last of the Five Good Emperors* of Rome.

Pax Romana. Rome expands from Scotland to the Middle East. Conquered people keep their native customs. Only the tribute—now paid to Rome—changes. Naturalization is granted. The Roman legal system serves all. Military patrols keep order. Legions defend Roman boundaries.

Culture undergoes a sweeping renaissance. Peace and prosperity ensue. The military is reorganized to circumvent civil war. As territorial gains are consolidated, battles of conquest cease. Trade in the Mediterranean booms.

Culture continues to prosper. Stability, and the time to enjoy it, are bountiful. With unprecedented internal and external peace, art and architecture flourish. Virgil pens the *Aeneid.* The Colosseum is built. Throughout Rome, culture's rewards are found in abundance.

Pax Romana. History would know it as Rome's greatest years.

~~~

Consultant: ***Culture*** *and* ***Training****. If you're weighing the importance of each, what would you give them?*

Leader: *50/50. Our people feeling connected is as important as their training.*

Consultant: *Tell me what you do for training.*

Leader: *Our team is the best trained in the industry. It's an ongoing process—we dedicate significant time and capital to their ongoing development. Meetings, lectures, workshops, e-learning, webinars, certifications, apps—we offer all of it. All state of the art. It's who we are.*

Consultant: *Very impressive training regime. Your team seem to know everything about your products and services.*

Leader: *Thank you. We know it's impressive.*

Consultant: *You mentioned **culture** being just as significant as training ... 50/50.*

Leader: *Yes—look around. Our people matter. They know we care.*

Consultant: *With culture mattering so much, what do you to promote it?*

Leader: ...

Consultant: *You **did** mention culture being as important as training, yes?*

Leader: *I did ...*

Consultant: *So much invested into training. What of culture?*

Leader: *... Nothing specific, we feel it's just part of the atmosphere. We strategize on our offerings, training, and customer experience. Culture isn't tangible. We can't measure it, and—in all honestly—we wouldn't know where to begin to.*

Consultant: *You aren't alone—few do. And those few are the very best in their business. Culture-focused organizations retain top talent, and build unstoppable teams.*

> **Let's get to work on yours.**

<p style="text-align:center">~~~</p>

Culture is far more than an esoteric, abstract concept. Antiquated organizations that miss this are behind in their industry—with the gap between winners and losers growing exponentially. High-impact cultures realize vast improvements in employee production, product quality, and positive customer response.

Culture is *not* a lofty, philosophical platitude. It is tangible. For the elite organization, *it is critical.*

~~~

In building culture, you must understand your audience.

Leaders, meet the *Millennials*—and the work environment they've inspired modern employees to seek. Modern employees do not say "Thank you" simply for having means to pay the bills. We aren't comfortable just being comfortable. We want **connection**, and **community**, and **meaningful work**. *If these are not valued in your organization, we'll walk out the door as fast as we walked in.*

Yes, product and service training are fundamental for elite organizations. This is not enough. Start with your mission statement. Go further.

Have colleagues write their own mission statements, encouraging ownership of their work. Get to know *their* values. Have personal mission statements written out, displayed at the colleague's work area. Let this be a source of tremendous pride. Have all write their mission statement on the same board. Place this board in a location seen by everyone daily. This makes culture tangible.

SHARE STORIES of core values in action. The Ritz-Carlton does this to incredible effect: In daily meetings, employees share stories of exceeding guest expectations. It is a daily cultural regime of discussing the values, living the values, and celebrating the values in action. Do the same. Weekly at the least—daily, much better. Start meetings with these potent, encouraging stories. Culture is not a switch. *Culture is an ongoing process.* Make these stories an evolving event; a powerful foundation—a rich tradition.

Leave room for fun. A 10-hour training day may seem to get a lot done—but it does not help retention. Many leaders fall for the myth of, *"Well, it was a lot, but we got it all in there."* No. You didn't. An endless training day is exhausting. It is disengaging. Colleagues will dread the experience. Try to cram in everything—they will remember nothing. Focused, concise, timely training will yield far better retention than an information avalanche. Temper training hours with social activities; breaks from the barrage allowing colleagues to relax and connect. Culture develops in the rhythm and cadence of training and social interaction. Both are critical.

Celebrate birthdays. Celebrate work anniversaries. Celebrate achieved goals. Celebrate colleagues going above and beyond. Go much further still. Weave these celebrations into the fabric of your culture. Frequency is far more important than grandeur—small, frequent celebrations far outweigh infrequent "grand" ones.

Again: today's employees want **connection**, and **community**, and **meaningful work**. As important as product and service training is culture. A united team is a successful team. Culture isn't about your offering or the competitive landscape. It's about your employees feeling important, unique, and valued. It's your interest in getting to know them, and encouraging them to get to know one another.

Stop viewing "people" as your greatest resource; every organization has "people". View the *connection of your people* as your greatest resource. This is where culture thrives. High-culture environments yield actively engaged members, driven to do their best for the group they so value. In business, sports, and life: When the pressure is on, the most knowledgeable team in the world will fall to the team connected through culture. Connected groups fight—and do not stop fighting.

~~~

Your greatest resource:

Your team's untapped engagement. *Culture.*

Rome's greatest years resulted from the strength of culture.

Redefine yours. Build *your* Pax Romana.

Look within.

Engagement is directly related to culture.

Improve culture, improve engagement.

Improve engagement, retain key talent and build an unstoppable team.

Retain key talent and build an unstoppable team—

Conquer the world.

There are no limits.

*"Is there anything worse for a state than to be split and disunited?
Or anything better than cohesion and unity?"*

—Plato

Predator: Honor the Unsung Heroes

The production proves horrendously challenging.

Schwarzenegger films in an unforgiving jungle. Temperatures are sweltering or freezing. Adjusting to the sloped terrain presents a constant, unbearable challenge—there is no real rest between takes. Logistics are a nightmare. Nothing is moved, executed, or accomplished with ease. Schwarzenegger, for the final scene alone, spends three weeks caked in mud battling *the Predator* in stagnant, foul, freezing water. Ultimately, Schwarzenegger's character Dutch emerges the hero.

Is Schwarzenegger the *real* hero of *Predator*? The answer is no.

Scenario

You, like all cast and crew, suffer through months of impossible filming conditions. It's a shared, mutual misery leaving none exempt. However, on top of these challenges, you must perform in a 200-pound Predator suit. It is hot and highly uncomfortable, worn for long hours and countless days. The suit is imbalanced, demanding constant effort to maintain any stance. You are unable to see out of the mask, requiring scenes to be fully re-hearsed before takes—*and performed from memory with no sensory perception.*

Meet Kevin Peter Hall. Hall stands a towering 7'2". He is a master of his craft—combining a degree in Theatrical Arts with professional experience in martial arts, basketball, and ballet. He is, in the purest form of the phrase, a one-of-a-kind talent.

Is Schwarzenegger's Dutch the hero of *Predator*? On the surface—yes. But who, dear reader, is the real hero? Whose sacrifice exceeds all others? *Who gave the most—and is recognized the least?*

Honor your unsung heroes.

Your assignment: Right now—*at this moment*—think of those whose contribution isn't in the spotlight. Those who are critical contributors to what you and your organization accomplish, ensuring success with little fanfare and tremendous vigilance. This morning, or afternoon, or Monday are fast approaching. *Thank these heroes.* Take the time, make an effort, and voice your appreciation. It absolutely matters.

They have earned it. You owe it. And everyone wins when you do.

> *"Victory in defeat, there is none higher. She didn't give up, Ben; she's still trying to lift that stone after it has crushed her. She's a father working while cancer eats away his insides, to bring home one more pay check. She's a twelve-year-old trying to mother her brothers and sisters because mama had to go to Heaven. She's a switchboard operator sticking to her post while smoke chokes her and fire cuts off her escape. She's all the unsung heroes who couldn't make it but never quit."*
>
> —Robert A. Heinlein,
> *Stranger in a Strange Land*

SECTION VI
MANAGING AN ORGANIZATION,
MANAGING YOUR LIFE

Napoleon Bonaparte:
Speed as a Force Multiplier

*"The strength of an army, like the amount of momentum in
mechanics, is estimated by mass times velocity. A swift march
enhances the morale of an army, increases its power for victory."*
—Napoleon Bonaparte

Napoleon is unstoppable. He will not fall. After relentless conquests, his
enemies understand none can face him alone—they must unify. Too much
power for one man; too upsetting to Europe's delicate balance. The Third
Coalition is born: an alliance between Great Britain, Austria, Russia,
Sweden, and Naples.

The Coalition forces march over the Rhine. With impossible speed,
Bonaparte's army counterattacks, shocking the unprepared invaders.
Overwhelmed and isolated, they are engulfed by Bonaparte's army. Yet,
many more Coalition armies remain on the march, pouring in from the
north and west. Bonaparte understands he must press the attack. A defen-
sive stance will not win the war—victory requires forcing the initiative.

Napoleon decides where he will make his stand: the town of Austerlitz.
Learning his intent, Coalition forces race to beat him there—and to stop
him from dictating the terms of the pending battle. The Coalition army
marches slowly; a single, cohesive, massive unit. Orders take hours to
communicate down the line.

None can match the speed of Napoleon. His *Grande Armée* is divided into individual Corps units—each a fully functioning, independent army; each an end unto itself. His Corps divide, move with unmatched speed and fluidity, and then converge at Austerlitz. Speed, yet again, rewards Bonaparte. Arriving at Austerlitz before the Allied forces, he personally—*to great advantage*—positions the battlefield on his terms.

Austerlitz. December 2, 1805.

As Coalition forces continue arriving and preparing for battle, Napoleon's army is prepared. They are fed, armed, and ready *now*. Napoleon engages Coalition forces from the north. Once battle lines are established, he feigns weakness in his army's right flank. Sensing collapse, Coalition forces engage the retreating French wing. In their scramble for a decisive victory, the Coalition overpursues; from discipline and order emerges complete chaos. Their line is now stretched dangerously thin—*exactly as Bonaparte anticipated*.

Through speed, Napoleon divides the enemy. Bonaparte successfully splits the Coalition army with a counterattack at their overstretched center. A crippling blow; the broken Coalition line cannot oppose the French divided. The end begins. Napoleon's Third Corps, a unit held in reserve, arrive after marching an unprecedented 70 miles *in two days*. The Coalition army—now surrounded, suffocating, and desperate—make an escape attempt across frozen lakes and ponds. Countless soldiers die as French artillery shatter the ice below them.

The Battle of Austerlitz is over. France's victory complete. French killed or captured: 9,000. Allied killed or captured: *four times as many—36,000*.

The leadership lesson is this.

Your competition is marching, preparing to steal your clients. To take your business. Waiting for you to fall behind; looking to get to the battlefield before you. And they are hungry. Inevitable shifts in the business landscape will always change client needs. There will *always* be new battlefields. You must *never* stop competing to keep your clients. You must obsessively anticipate their needs—*and get there first*.

It's you or the competition; one will win—one will lose. Whoever identifies and adapts to change; whoever researches, plans, and prepares for evolving client needs; whoever obsessively scans the horizon for challenges and opportunities—*and gets there first*—will win.

~~~

"Speed as a Force Multiplier: A capability that, when added to and employed by a combat force, significantly increases the combat potential of that force and thus enhances the probability of successful mission accomplishment."

~~~

Bonaparte's lesson:

Speed gets you there first.

Get there first, and you dictate the terms.

Dictate the terms, and you hold the initiative.

Hold the initiative, and you win.

"To suffer the penalty of too much haste, which is too little speed."

—Plato

Spielberg: Launch Your Career

Filmmakers strive for a hit so successful that they are granted complete artistic control of future projects. Few succeed. A notable exception: Steven Spielberg. After early success with *The Sugarland Express,* Spielberg's star is rising. His next project: *Jaws.* He is 27 years old.

Filming is a disaster. The mechanized shark malfunctions, untested in salt water. Ocean conditions are unforgiving. *Jaws* is the first major film to be shot on the ocean, and unanticipated problems crop up every single day. Loaded with expensive equipment, the boat begins sinking *at the wrong time.* The crew scramble to save gear. A reel of film is retrieved from the water. The production is challenged in every way a production can be challenged. Frustrated cast and crew call the film *"Flaws."* A 55-day shoot turns into a 159-day nightmare. Young Spielberg's rising star is falling.

Until *Jaws* hit theaters. The movie: Over 67 million moviegoers. Acclaim from critics and fans alike. A global sensation; *the highest grossing film of all time.* The "summer blockbuster" is born. 27-year-old Spielberg shakes the very roots of the industry.

Spielberg could have thrown up his hands, cutting his losses and submitting an inferior film. Instead, he demanded—and got—the time and money to get it right. He took full advantage of the delays, using them as an opportunity to rewrite the script into the masterpiece of suspense we know today.

His lesson: Be *uncompromising* in the quality of your early work, which establishes momentum for the career to follow. The faster a rocket leaves the atmosphere, the further it goes. You must approach your career with the same mindset.

In the early years, *work twice as hard as you think you should.* Family first, in everything always. You steal no time, focus, or attention from your loved ones. At all other times—you are at the grindstone. Others can spend their early years in worthless pursuits of leisure. Your time is invested in *your future.* You'll be over a horizon they will never see.

These benefits compound over your entire career. Whether 20 days or 20 years in, start now. Like saving for retirement, it is never too late to begin. Your knowledge, skills, work ethic, toughness, tenacity, and humility will define those sacred early years. Invest in each fully. Accolades of early success fuel confidence and momentum. They stay with you. They belong to you. *They are part of you.*

Results of Spielberg's extraordinary career launch:

The Sugarland Express

Jaws

Close Encounters of the Third Kind

Raiders of the Lost Ark

E.T. the Extra-Terrestrial

Indiana Jones and the Temple of Doom

The Color Purple

The Goonies

Empire of the Sun

Always

Indiana Jones and the Last Crusade

Hook

Jurassic Park

Schindler's List

Amistad

Saving Private Ryan

A.I. Artificial Intelligence

Minority Report

Catch Me If You Can

The Terminal

War of the Worlds

Flags of Our Fathers

Letters from Iwo Jima

Lincoln

In Spielberg's own words:

> *"You have many years ahead of you to create the dreams that we can't even imagine dreaming."*

Launch strong. *You will get there*.

> *"No good ending can be expected in the absence of the right beginning."*
>
> —I Ching

Alexander the Great: Work, Life, and Balance

336 BC. *The Kingdom of Macedon—Ancient Greece.*

Philip II, King of Macedon, is assassinated. His son Alexander—tutored by Aristotle—is well versed in philosophy and military strategy. Alexander ascends the throne. His animosity toward Philip, a heavy drinker and degenerate, fuels his passion for glory. He will not stand in the shadow of his father, who favored diplomacy. He will rule with sword and spear. He will forge his own path. His vision: conquer to the *"ends of the world and the Great Outer Sea."* Immediately he quells several revolts, consolidating his power—and launching a campaign to conquer the Persian Empire.

334 BC. *War.*

Alexander marches, his vast army more than 48,000 soldiers and 6,000 cavalry strong. He defeats the Persian army at *The Battle of the Granicus River.* He defeats them at Issus—the beginning of the end of the Persian empire. The port city of Tyre falls. The stronghold of Gaza will not stand. Alexander is unstoppable.

The Battle of Gaugamela.

Alexander crosses the Tigris and Euphrates unopposed. King Darius III himself leads the Persian army. The Macedonian forces, heavily concentrated in a wedge-shaped phalanx, pierce the Persian center. Darius's charioteer dies in the melee. Persian troops believe King Darius has fallen. Chaos ensues. The Persian lines break. Darius flees. The battle is over.

The loss at Gaugamela shatters the spine of Persian resistance. Victory abounds; relentless momentum achieved. Asia Minor. Syria. Egypt. Babylonia. Persia. All conquered.

Onward to India.

For Alexander, these victories are not enough. He marches his army into India, ruthlessly slaughtering all resistance while reducing opposing strongholds to rubble.

Battle of the Hydaspes.

Alexander battles King Porus of the Paurava Kingdom. Porus's massive army, including charioteers and war elephants, ultimately falls. While a victory, the losses to Alexander and his companion cavalry are devastating. King Porus's resistance is unmatched among Alexander's previous conquests.

Revolt.

Alexander's army has had enough. *This war is endless.* His soldiers are exhausted; weary. Alexander tries to push them on—but they refuse. *Ten years of this.* It was time to turn back west. Back to family. *Back to home.* And so, the campaign ends. They never lost a single battle.

They walked away from the war.

~~~

"Burnout: physical or mental collapse caused by overwork or stress."

~~~

We are killing ourselves.

The stress of work compounds the harder we push, and the longer we go, without rest and recuperation. The toll overworking takes is overwhelming. Welcome to being human: No amount of willpower will overcome an endless barrage of *chronic stress*. None are exempt from this universal biological rule. Our hormones desperately attempt to manage our stress levels. Cortisol and epinephrine flood the system, pushing us from fight to flight. Praying for a reprieve.

There is an answer.

75% of regular vacationers feel more alert upon returning to work. Nearly 20% report an improved sleep cycle.

Adrenal dysfunction from chronic stress reduces the body's ability to fight illness. Testosterone levels lower, not only reducing the willpower for sex—but the physiological response required for it. Vacationers show increased levels of glucose, meaning not only more energy—but a reduction in weight as well. A devastating statistic: Regular vacationers are up to 50% *less likely* to have a stress-induced heart attack. Stress fuels high blood pressure. Stress fuels heart disease. The cardiologic response that stress provokes prematurely ends lives. Again: We are killing ourselves.

The leadership lesson is this.

Step away. Back off. Recalibrate. Recharge. *Take a vacation*. Vacations increase overall happiness. They reduce hormones that cause depression and anxiety. Vacations strengthen marriages and bond families. They slow the biological aging process.

What this means for you, dear leader: with vacation time taken, *employee production increases*. They give more—and you get more—when routinely encouraged to step away. Your team needs a break. They need rest and recuperation. The human animal operates within biologic limitations. No matter how pressing the project, how important the initiative—burnout is inevitable. We can only push so hard for so long. For them—*and you*—balancing the work/life cycle is critical.

Take a vacation. *Encourage the employee reluctant to do so.* Share the health benefits. Explain the productivity benefits. Step away. Everybody wins.

Alexander never lost a battle, *but he never stopped fighting them.* For his soldiers, ten years of endless military conquest. *Ten years.* No rest. No reprieve. No chance to enjoy the love of family and the comforts of home. Absolute burnout. His soldiers were done. *No more.*

Alexander's army turned their back on him.

If you don't pull back, *so will yours*.

"If you want to change the world, go home and love your family."
—Mother Teresa,
nun and missionary

Wall Street: On Money

Wall Street.

Bud Fox, a rookie New York stock broker, idolizes Gordon Gekko—a soulless business icon living by the mantra *"Greed is good."* Intoxicated by Gekko's money, status, and power, Bud seeks mentorship. He earns the opportunity. Bud absorbs Gekko's corrupt ways, abandoning ethics entirely.

Bud is betrayed.

Gekko exploits Bud, manipulating a shut-down of Bud's father's airline. Promises were made—jobs would be secure; the company would remain operational. These promises are broken. Bud counter-punches, manipulating the stock to protect the airline, secure the workforce, and punish Gekko financially. It works, though Bud is quickly caught and sentenced to jail. The final blow is his—Bud records a conversation as Gekko confesses everything. The authorities strike immediately.

Ironically, *Wall Street* arrives shortly before the October 1987 stock market crash known as *Black Monday*—a 22% one day drop in the Dow Jones Industrial Average.

Ultimately, *Wall Street* is entertaining. Its thesis, however, is wrong. *Money is not greed.* Money is **freedom**. Money is **opportunity**. We are ingrained with the belief that money is immoral. Money is "the root of all evil". The reality is quite different: Money is a tool of exchange; nothing more—a tool that positive progress demands.

You *must* outgrow the belief financial prosperity is an unethical goal. Your income is a direct result of the value you add to others; the more you are making—*the more value you are giving*. This should be a tremendous source of pride. *Not shame.*

~~~

The Engine of Compound Interest

Dear twenty-something: If you will hold out on a status symbol car, we just earned you 1.5 million dollars.

Here's how.

We'll assume a car payment of $450 a month. For the average consumer, this is a lifelong expense; the thrill of a new vehicle every few years meaning constant automobile debt.

We're not going to buy a new car. We're going to buy a practical, reliable vehicle with the cash that would have been a down payment on a car—or skip buying a car entirely, using electric transportation, carpooling, and Uber as needed. If living, working, and attending class within a three-mile radius, a bike is far more convenient than the car you don't need.

We're going to take our $450 a month and begin investing. For this example, we'll forecast an 8% annual growth rate, starting at age 25. The S&P index, historically, doubles just over every six years. The years go by. The money builds. And *builds*. And BUILDS. Through the engine of compounding interest, at age 65, your investment is worth *1.5 million dollars*.

We just bought future you a house. A grandchild's college tuition. The means to travel anywhere you want. *The means to live any way you want.* Define your vision on your terms. Start investing now, and it will be yours.

Back to the car you want, but don't need. Those high-status rides on the showroom floor certainly look nice. How easy it is to get caught in the fever of "*I deserve this*," "*I work hard enough*," "*You only live once*," and other such pacifying logic masking a horrendous, emotional impulse to buy.

Before signing the loan on an unnecessary status symbol, tell yourself this: *Nobody else gives a shit. No one is impressed. No one cares. No one but you.* And six weeks after the purchase, you won't either. The magic quickly fades away. *The payments do not.* No pouring your money into a depreciating asset. Put that same money to work building the freedom that future-you deserves.

Form this habit *now*: Invest 15% of every dollar you make. Do so religiously, and future you is an automatic millionaire.

The 15% rule is not just for twenty-somethings. Younger; older—it does not matter. The right time to make 15% a habit is *now*. Time is wealth's greatest ally. Leverage every moment.

~~~

> "*It's a zero-sum game—somebody wins, somebody loses. Money itself isn't lost or made, it's simply transferred—from one perception to another.*"
>
> —Gordon Gekko

~~~

Gordon Gekko is wrong: money is *not* a zero-sum game. A rising economic tide lifts all boats. Stock dividend payouts add new wealth to the economy.

*Money is **not** a finite resource.* Time, however, *is*. Nothing matches the power of time in guaranteeing financial success.

The same is true of leadership. Building trust and passion in a team does not happen overnight—but once you do start, that trust and commitment compounds over time. Investing in stocks might require startup capital, but no matter how much money you have, you can invest in developing yourself as a leader *today*.

Every day that you do not maximize your leadership potential is a day you will never get back.

Turning back to finance, the universal truth is clear: Our time here is limited. Money isn't greed. Money is the freedom to use our most precious asset—our time—*as we see fit.* The freedom to live a life rich in purpose and meaning *defined on our terms.*

The most effective philanthropists in the world didn't do it by asking others for money—they did it by the fruits of their labor, the generosity of their souls, and the wisdom of thinking long-term.

Money is **freedom**. Money is **opportunity**.

Future-you deserves both.

> *"The importance of money flows from it being a link between the present and the future."*
>
> —John Maynard Keynes

Up in the Air: The Art of Living

Meet Ryan Bingham: a traveling businessman who calls life in the air *"home."* While his work as a "Termination Engineer" is brutal and depressing, he embodies the jet-set lifestyle. Luxury lounges, executive suites, the best of everything. All of the external status symbols of happiness and success.

Quickly, the spell is broken. We see Ryan for what he is: *alone*. The superficially glamorous lifestyle reveals a life of hollow perks, meaningless goals, and no authentic human connection. Ryan's philosophy is simple: Material goods are baggage. People are baggage. Freedom and happiness come through having no obligations to anything—or anyone. *Keep your backpack empty.*

Ryan will commit to nothing, and he attracts a love interest personifying what he *thinks* he wants; casual, non-committal; carefree. Ryan begins to see what he's missing. Through his colleague Natalie Keeler and his romance with fellow business traveler Alex Goran, Ryan questions his philosophy of *freedom through solitude.*

Ryan's catharsis occurs at his sister's wedding. His family speak candidly: No one hears from him. No one sees him. He's never around. It is fairly assumed he doesn't want to be. In speaking with his future brother-in-law, who is questioning life and marriage, Ryan must confront his own beliefs:

"If you think about it, your favorite memories, the most important moments of your life ... Were you alone? Life's better with company."

The film's ending disappoints many viewers expecting a check-the-box finale where everything falls into place. This is not the ending presented; we are instead exposed to the natural consequences of Ryan's philosophy. Alex sought the same terms Ryan initially offered. It is Ryan—after his awakening—who tries to incite change in an impossible situation. We learn she is married.

In the final scene, Ryan flies yet again, leaving the viewer unsure whether any meaningful growth has occurred. *And there, it ends.* Did Ryan change? We don't know. Those frustrated with the film's ambiguous ending are missing the point. The message was not for Clooney's Ryan Bingham.

The message is for you.

Ryan's experience reflects that of many: the same airports. The same hotels. The same pseudo-hospitality. The same pursuit of meaningless status through superficial perks. The same four walls. The same hotel bar. Everything the same. Night after night, year after year.

~~~

The dilemma:

1) The challenges—and vulnerability—of authentic human connection.

2) The freedom—and isolation—of a life lived alone.

As gambling is to the gambling addict, or alcohol to the alcoholic, Ryan's preoccupation with jet-setting is an attempt to fill the void of authentic relationships in his life.

The Art of Living:

Embracing the challenges of healthy relationships.

Accepting that people need people.

And that no one can do it alone.

The life well lived rejects the dead-end road of isolation. The life well lived is defined by authentic human connection. The personal counseling profession is built on this premise: At the heart of every broken person is a broken relationship. A family member, friend, spouse; someone who should have been there wasn't—or isn't. This is *always* the source. Healing begins with awareness, coping strategies, and the slow march of time.

Take inventory.

If your relationships are not healthy, or are nonexistent, *now* is the time to change. Fight for a marriage worth fighting for. Talk to the family you haven't spoken with in years. Get the counseling you need.

Apologize to those you should apologize to. **Bury it.**

In the short term, none of this is easy. In the long term, **it will reshape your world.**

Now get to it.

> *"If you have it [Love], you don't need to have anything else, and if you don't have it, it doesn't matter much what else you have."*
>
> —Sir James M. Barrie

Citizen Kane: On Raising Children

Rosebud is the answer. *Watch* Citizen Kane *for the question.*

~~~

Citizen Kane; 1941. Co-written, directed, produced, and starred in by 25-year-old Orson Welles. Ponder the scope of this achievement: four primary functions mastered by one filmmaker, committed to—and successful in—making an absolute masterpiece. How good is *Citizen Kane?*

American Film Institute's 100 Greatest American Movies of All Time: #1. **Citizen Kane.**

~~~

In his childhood, Charles Kane's family discover gold on their land. His parents want a "better life" for him. He is taken from his home, sent to distant boarding schools, and given an extensive formal education ensuring a lifetime of "success." Thus, Kane's childhood is taken from him. His connection with his parents is over.

In adulthood there is no material possession Kane doesn't have. He runs his own newspaper. His palatial estate in Florida, *Xanadu*, has endless rooms, lavish gardens, a hoard of fine art; all the amenities of wealth and privilege.

Ultimately, the loss of home and childhood leave a hole in Kane impossible to fill. And then he dies *very much alone,* though he is surrounded by staff. Never truly happy; never once *complete.*

~~~

On Raising Children

Imagine an island. *It is solely yours.*

Imagine every material possession you could possibly desire. Anything at any time. Exotic cars. A casino. A roller coaster. Money. Jewels. Name it. It's yours. Let your imagination wander—everything you want is there; anything you want later will be there. Think it, and it is yours. There is, however, one condition. *It's just you on the island. No one else—now or ever.*

Imagine a summer evening.

The sun is setting. Food is laid out on a picnic table; the grill is fired up. The old tell stories while the young listen. Others throw a ball back and forth. A guitar, slightly out of tune, is strummed. Friends. Family. Loved ones. All are here. Nothing extravagant. Nothing opulent. Just communion with those you cherish.

Two scenarios.

The first: every material desire you want. The very best of everything that money can provide. *But entirely alone.* The second: no material possessions, though surrounded by family, friends, and loved ones, fully immersed in the pleasures of simple living. I would ask you to choose one of the two scenarios—but you've already made your decision.

Quality vs. Quantity

This is a myth. Time with your children being either quality *or* quantity, but not possibly both, is an absurd notion. It's an excuse parents not prioritizing time with family give themselves—and it is a false one.

Some children, on occasion, get a splashy event with their parents. Usually a birthday or holiday; at times something spontaneous. But always big and memorable and expensive. One tailor-made for a photo op—an envy-inducing experience proudly displayed on Facebook.

These children are often the busiest you'll ever meet. A nanny—sometimes nannies—tend to their every need. As they grow up, they are gifted with endless opportunities: tutors, sports, rehearsals, recitals, on and on. Never a moment wasted—each experience rolling into the next. On the rare occasion the family is home together, they're little more than ships passing in the night.

If this is your concept of raising children, *change the paradigm immediately*. Truly unconditional love and authentic connection will take your children much further in life than the endless regime of activities associated with "privilege." Home needs to be a harbor. Go out and conquer the world today—knowing the unconditional love of family awaits you right here—*and it always will*. Give your children all the time and focused attention you possibly can. Make home a haven.

Three key words: balance, presence, routine.

Balance.

Balance the activities of your family. A sport or hobby is healthy and positive, modeling the values of hard work, success, and overcoming failure. Potent teaching tools. The challenge comes when there's no time—or room—for anything else. Keep the activity volume modest and manageable. *Family first—in everything, always.*

Presence.

Granting undivided attention can be very challenging. It isn't just you—this is a universal truth. Gone are the days of work being at work—and left at work—after 5:00. Our phones. Our laptops. We are *constantly* connected. We feel tethered to our profession; never more than an email or phone call away from being needed. In time and attention, technology has taken far more from us than it has given.

Try this. Leave the laptop at the office. Leave the phone in the car. When you pull into the driveway, you *check out* of work, thoughts of work, lingering projects at work, pressing responsibilities at work—all of it. It is a mindset. It is a habit. It is a decision. *It will work.*

Walk to the door. Leave *every thought of work* behind. You now *check into* being the husband, wife, mother, or father your family needs you to be. They are waiting for you. And they deserve your very best. Open the door. Watch how powerful the change is when family isn't competing for your attention—when you are home, nothing else in the world matters beyond them. And they are always first.

Routine.

Build time as a family into your daily schedule. Breakfast in the morning; everyone prepares to launch their day together. A family dinner in the evening. A daily activity in the yard, or a board game. It can be any or all of these, but must be—*at the very least*—once daily.

Turn the television off.

Time together should be in conversation, or bonding over a mutually enjoyable activity. When the television is on, it gets the attention that should be shared between the family.

~~~

Citizen Kane masterfully teaches this truth: Lonely success will never compare to the warmth of a loving, connected family. No amount of privileged living will *ever* yield a fulfilled life.

Family engagement is not an on/off switch—it is a spectrum to which we parents must constantly be attuned. So absorbed in our professions, we often lose perspective; our preoccupation with work stifling our time with family and children. Physically we may be here, though mentally we're *there*. We aren't truly present in the moment. We must consistently evaluate this paradigm, combating an unconscious problem with a conscious solution: *Leave work at work*. When at home with family, they get 100% without compromise.

Additionally, many are victims of a parenting cycle never providing the authentic connection all children need. We naturally model the patterns we were given, unaware we are doing so—and unaware of the consequences. If you are a victim of such an upbringing, let this be the moment awareness incites change. Let yours be the generation that, in your family, breaks the cycle.

It starts today. Leave the laptop. Turn off the phone. Open the door.

They are waiting for you.

> *"Life affords no greater responsibility, no greater privilege, than the raising of the next generation."*
>
> —C. Everett Koop

The Godfather: On Retirement

Yes, financial discipline and literacy are crucial for retirement, and yet, there is something far more important. It is about numbers. *It is not about money.* The greatest business lesson isn't even about business. It's about life, and the years to come.

The Math

Average Retirement Age: *63*

Average Life Expectancy: *79*

Post-Retirement Years: 16

Contemplate this. Make these years yours. Think of the life you've led since 2003 (*16 years prior to this writing*). The highs, the lows, those who have come, those who have gone—the events, the people, the places, the pivotal moments—*all of it*. The same amount of time awaits in retirement.

The Movie

The key conflict of *The Godfather* series is brilliantly depicted in one scene: Michael outdoors in his chair, sitting in isolated silence amongst the falling leaves, after selling his soul for business, power, and position. His face a mask of tortured silence—a man incapable of escaping himself. His thoughts linger on all he has done.

Michael literally, and metaphorically, closed the door on Kay. Business over family.

He betrayed the wishes of his father, Don Corleone:

"I never wanted this for you. I worked my whole life—I don't apologize—to take care of my family, and I refused to be a fool, dancing on the string held by all those bigshots. I don't apologize—that's my life—but I thought that, that when it was your time, that you would be the one to hold the string. Senator Corleone; Governor Corleone."

Michael's response: *"We'll get there, Pop. We'll get there."* All that follows betrays the Don's plea; Michael is intoxicated by power and unwilling to abandon the old ways.

Most tragic of all, the murder—in cold blood—of his own brother Fredo. *"I know it was you, Fredo. You broke my heart. You broke my heart."* Michael is unable to forgive; unwilling to understand. Power over family.

The Lesson

What will matter most during your 16 years? For all of us, those years are fast approaching. *Far faster than we realize.* The purpose and pride of a career doing what you love is critical for the life well lived. Financial security as well.

Neither is the most important investment. The devastating consequences of an unhealthy work/life balance are well known. We can all cite examples we have witnessed. Broken marriages, time and distance from friends and family, memories missed with the children who arrive, stay, and then embark on their own lives. Countless moments that can never be replaced.

Family first—in everything, always.

Citizen Kane teaches us the value of meaningfully engaging with our children—at all times, in all ways. But the principle is not limited to raising children. *Family first* means continuing that relationship with your adult children, and investing just as heavily in your other relationships—with siblings, with extended family, with your own parents. Retirement's greatest gift is the time it allows us to do just that.

When the sun sets for each of us, it won't be a job we reflect on—it will be the love of those who surround us and care for us, who love us and whom we love in return. *That* will be the legacy you leave. You will be sixteen years removed from your professional life. *Sixteen years.*

Family first—in everything, always.

The Godfather films are a cautionary tale for each of us. Once again consider Michael Corleone, alone in his chair, contemplating the devastating choices he has made. Michael is haunted by the tragedy of all he has done; the monster he has become. He has failed, and knows it. He will sit in that chair alone. *And Forever.*

Family first—in everything, always.

"Blood is thicker than water."
—12th century German proverb

Arete: Defining Leadership

Arete. Though no exact translation exists in English, the words closest to the Greek term *Arete* are *excellence* and *moral virtue*. *Arete* is the greatness of a thing in relation to its potentiality. It's the *greatness* of a blade's cut. It's the *greatness* of a singer's voice. It's the *greatness* of a leader's ability to inspire.

Arete in Leadership

Through Aristotle, the concept of Arete in leadership is brilliantly illustrated. He defines the two key components of high-quality leadership: **Competence** and **Character**. *Arete* in leadership requires both.

Between competence and character, competence is most easily defined. Qualified leadership demands an understanding of the tools, skills, knowledge, and resources needed to execute the organization's initiatives. The greatest leader in the world is rendered ineffective when tasked to lead an endeavor of which they know nothing. Others will not—*and should not*—follow.

A *competent* leader with mastery of the task earns the right to lead; this is the cost of entry. To lead effectively, the leader must demonstrate exemplary *character*. Character, as defined in Greek philosophy, is characterized by four cardinal virtues: *Wisdom, justice, courage, and moderation.*

Arete in leadership develops when guided by *wisdom* of circumstances and opportunities. When *justice*—fairness and equality for all—are exercised.

When *courage*, fearlessness in the face of challenge, is demonstrated. When *moderation*—leadership untethered to the base desires of status, money, sex, or power—is exemplified.

Arete in leadership is then seen for what it is: an ongoing, never-ending *process*. The wise, just, courageous, and moderate leader doesn't check a box to establish authority—he or she demonstrates the cardinal virtues relentlessly in word, action, and deed.

New leader, before your journey begins, ask yourself:

1) Am I competent in the task? Leaders who don't know their stuff aren't leaders. Establish the credibility your role requires.

2) How will I demonstrate *wisdom, justice, courage*, and *moderation* in all things?

Strategize; contemplate. Discuss with established leaders in your field and organization. The greatest leaders are also the greatest students. *Become one.* So many new leaders believe they've finally "arrived," oblivious to the truth: *They have not yet started.* Do not be one of them. True leaders understand what leadership is not: *privilege*. True leaders understand the burden of leadership, and the enormous responsibilities the role requires.

So many endeavors fail in the margin between decent leadership and **true** leadership. **You are a true leader**. This is your roadmap.

Arete—excellence; moral virtue. There is power in this concept; it applies uniquely to each situation. At the family dinner table, in the classroom, at the corporate meeting, at team practice, define *Arete* for each role within the organization.

Telling your team to do *"a great job"* isn't leadership. It's garbage. Effective leadership defines *Arete* within a role, establishing the tasks each requires for greatness. Effective leadership says, "Greatness will be achieved through x, y, and z," a predefined, deeply considered plan tailored to each division—and each team member's role within that division. Define what greatness looks like—*Arete*—and *then* inspire.

You are a true leader. You demonstrate competency in the task. This opens the door. Along the journey, you ceaselessly model *wisdom, justice, courage, and moderation*. Do this, and they will follow you into the trenches. Do this, and they will bleed for a worthy cause.

Do this, and you are leadership defined.

> *"I am not afraid of an army of lions led by a sheep; I am afraid of an army of sheep led by a lion."*
>
> —Alexander the Great

King Henry V: Where Leaders Stand

October, 1415. Northern France.

The Hundred Years' War between England and France rages on. King Henry and the English, comprised mostly of longbowmen, are outnumbered three to one. Their numbers are decimated by disease and dysentery. Food is so scarce soldiers eat leaves to survive.

Marching for the safety of English-held Calais, the French intercept the English. There is no going back. There is no going forward. Battle is imminent. King Henry orders that none speak a word this night. They rest, solemn and composed—preparing for the battle to come.

Knights from across France have taken arms against the English invaders. They seek valor through *the code of chivalry,* a system of bravery, honor, courtesy, service, and gallantry. Under the code, nothing is more sacred than glory in battle. Each soldier arrives to claim theirs.

While the English sit in silence, the French camp is alive with activity. French soldiers mock King Henry. They drink. They celebrate. They savor the victory to come. Their enemy: outnumbered, outmatched. *Desperate.*

The Battle of Agincourt begins.

Henry's archers taunt the French, baiting them into an undisciplined charge. They wave two fingers at the enemy lines, a mockery of the French threats to cut the bow firing fingers off every English captive. The ploy works. Without orders, the cavalry begin the march. An ocean of French soldiers thunders toward the English.

Exactly as King Henry wanted.

The English longbowmen deliver a murderous barrage of arrows. Between the confines of the wooded battlefield, the French cannot flank English archers. The bulk of their army advance forward, pushing those in front into slaughter. France's predicted victory proves a disaster. *It gets far worse.*

~~~

Weeks of rain have softened the battlefield. The French knight's greatest asset—their heavy armor—is now their greatest liability. Knocked into the mud, the knights cannot stand back up. Men suffocate. Men are trampled. Horses go berserk. The French attack is reduced to chaos.

The English ultimately win. To prevent any French rally, French prisoners are put to the sword. The pride of France lay at Henry's feet. *More than 8,000 dead*; France's Admiral. France's Constable. Eight counts. A viscount. Three dukes. *Thousands of soldiers.*

600 years later, Agincourt remains one of England's most celebrated victories. *How did this happen?* For the French: Pride. Arrogance. Adherence to an antiquated "chivalric" code of conduct. France's King Charles VI did not, as was customary, stay at the rear of his army—in a fit of madness, *he is not there at all.*

For the English: Superior battlefield positioning. The strength of the English longbow. And above all of these, *one of history's greatest leaders*: King Henry V.

King Henry fights at the front of the battle, so close to the action that a jewel on his crown is sheared off. He understands that if he falls, the French will win. He also understands that leading the English to victory will require every resource available—*including the possibility of losing his life.*

Henry would lead his men to victory—or die alongside them as equals. Not behind them, giving orders. *With them*, sword drawn, at the front lines. Yes, their King—but also, *their kin*.

The force of King Henry's leadership carries the day. The English win an impossible victory. King Henry V, *leading from the front*, is the reason why.

> *"This story shall the good man teach his son;*
> *And Crispin Crispian shall ne'er go by,*
> *From this day to the ending of the world,*
> *But we in it shall be remembered-*
> *We few, we happy few, we band of brothers"*
> —*Henry V*; William Shakespeare

The leadership lesson is this.

Too many leaders are comfortable maintaining the status quo, removed from the battle; giving orders from the back. Without King Henry's bold leadership at the front, the English would have lost. Leaders:

The engagement, growth, and success of those in your charge is the *exact* measure of the quality of your leadership.

It's easy when times are good. It feels sufficient to lead from the back. Leadership's *real* test: What will you do when times are tough? When the challenges seem insurmountable? When the team is up against the ropes? Are you behind your soldiers, *or with them*?

Your battle is coming.

You, like King Henry, *must* stand at the front with your soldiers. The extra hours. The relentless effort. Not leadership through words: vague, meaningless. *Leadership through action*. You are unwavering in your commitment to your team. You are *lethal* in your execution against competitors.

The competition stand on the other side of the battlefield. They are the enemy. We're not here to play nice. We're not here to get along. We are here to beat you. Destroy you. **Annihilate you.**

Leadership from the back works through the modern chivalric code of *"plenty of business for everyone."* We're doing *well enough.* We're comfortably sufficient, *but far from great.* To hell with that code. If comfortable is good enough, *you are not doing your job.* Henry won his war because he abandoned the knight's chivalric code, doing what must be done to win.

You must do the same.

You approach business with a warfare mentality. You are your team's leader. There, at the front, sword and shield in hand. Rallying your troops.

You were hired to win. **You are paid to win. Win.**

When others arrive, they will ask where you are.

Your team will answer:

*There—as always—***right at the front.**

> *"Leadership is a two-way street, loyalty up and loyalty down. Respect for one's superiors; care for one's crew."*
>
> —Grace Hopper

Leadership: Don't Be a Dick Jones

There are robots. There are cops. Then, there are **RoboCops.**

~~~

Meet **Dick Jones**, executive at Omni Consumer Products. Dick offers a simple, practical solution to the burgeoning crime problem that plagued Detroit in the 1980s: *Robots.*

During a live demonstration at an executive board meeting Dick's robot inadvertently kills an innocent bystander, firing thousands of bullets in 3.4 seconds. Criminal or otherwise, this many rounds to stop one guy does seem excessive. If taxpayers have to shell out eleven grand in munitions every time Dick's robot stops a crime, the city will go bankrupt.

Dick isn't the only one with an affinity for robotic police officers, and, *without seeking approval from his executive board,* orders the grisly assassination of his internal rival's robo-inspired anti-crime-bot. Dick loves *his* robot. There will be no other.

Dick is ultimately exposed for what he is: a horrible boss. Not only does he have fellow executives killed, he also treats the half-man, half-machine *RoboCop* Murphy with absolute disdain:

"What did you think? That you were an ordinary police officer?
You're our product, and we can't very well have our products turning
against us, can we?"

Without hardworking, blue-collar *RoboCops* like Murphy, Dick would be out of his privileged executive job. Dick has no gratitude or camaraderie with robo-people—only disdain. Dick might be "the boss," *but Dick is no leader.* Dick is clueless about motivating employees. Robo-folk and human alike, it makes no difference:

Disdain is a leadership killer.

Understand: People do not quit companies.

People quit bad leaders.

To retain premium talent, *DO* be a leader. *DON'T* be a Dick. *Here's how.*

~~~

Wait 24 hours. *Sleep on it.*

When challenging circumstances arise, emotions immediately take over. *The control you think you have, you do not.*

This trap is well known by parents: The child does something wrong, the parent responds too impulsively, emotions cause an overreaction, the overreaction becomes its own problem—often a *bigger* problem than the original issue itself.

Leaders: *wait.*

Give it a day. Give it a good night's sleep. Your emotions will settle. Your better judgement will rise.

Then, proceed.

Correcting Behavior and Natural Consequences

Instead of "punishment," speak of *natural consequences*. This is a *critical* concept. *Natural consequences* result from consistent patterns of behavior. We identify, and course-correct, behavior whose *natural consequences* cost your reputation. Or career. Or marriage. *Or life.* These are the ongoing patterns that, when played to their natural conclusion, will end with devastating results. They may be an ongoing action, habit, relationship, belief, or vice.

Note the application: this is not *"punishment"*. This is recognizing a behavior pattern that, should it carry on, will end with devastating consequences. We must not shy away from these discussions, be them at work, at home, or otherwise. We do this from authentic care and concern, and in doing so: The message will *not* be, *"I'm in charge and because I said so."*

It *will* be, *"I care for you, and I need you to see where this behavior pattern ends."* We're stopping a tragedy before it happens.

Masking Anger and Disappointment

Start the discussion with this: *"I feel."* *"I feel disappointed when you don't do what you said you would do."* *"I feel angry when you said the team can count on you, but you didn't show up."* This phrase lays a safe, solid foundation to build the conversation upon. This keeps the interaction from feeling like an attack. We are not entering a war, nor seeking to start one. *I feel* cannot be disputed or argued, and lowers the other's defenses.

Equally important: not pretending you aren't affected by what has occurred. Faking indifference doesn't help anyone. They need to understand the consequences their actions have on others. And they need to see you address those consequences in a reasonable, rational, controlled manner (which you will do—*24 hours later*).

~~~

Don't be a Dick Jones. **Be a leader.**

Wait to respond. Speak in terms of *natural consequences.* Start with *"I feel".* Do not feign indifference—be honest, direct; *sincere.* Put these principles to work. They will work for you.

Then witness the power of authentic, positive change.

> *"If your action inspires others to dream more, learn more, do more*
> *and become more you are a leader."*
>
> —John Quincy Adams

Muhammad Ali: Survive the Storm

October 30, 1974. Kinshasa, Zaire. *The Rumble in the Jungle.*

Muhammad Ali battles undefeated George Foreman for the world heavyweight championship. 60,000 attend the live event. Over *one billion* watch on television. It would later be called *"the greatest sporting event of the 20th century."* History has proven this to be true.

Coming off a loss to Joe Frazier, former heavyweight champion Muhammad Ali enters the fight a 4-1 underdog. The boxing world predicts an inevitable outcome—the hard-hitting George Foreman, who defeated Joe Frazier in *two rounds*, will crush a past-his-prime Ali. A swift finish is anticipated.

As was Ali's custom, leading up to the fight, he provokes his opponent. He states his speed will be Foreman's downfall. The goal: Lure Foreman into an angry, over-aggressive response that ultimately plays to Ali's advantage.

It works.

Anticipating Ali's strategy of a fast, clean fight Foreman prepares for a flurry of punches; Ali operating at maximum speed. *Foreman gets something very different.* Ali knew a toe-to-toe battle did not favor him. Heavy-hitting Foreman could finish him with one well-placed shot. Ali would not give him the fight he expected. The key: Let Foreman wear himself down. Let him unleash his barrage of devastating punches early in the fight.

Ali must survive the storm.

Ali's strategy is revealed; the now famous *rope-a-dope* tactic. Back against the ropes, Ali taunts Foreman into punching him. Ali defends his face, taking Foreman's heavy shots in the midsection. The ropes themselves help absorb the impact. Ali gives Foreman no window to land a knockout shot to the head.

> *"After three rounds, I had hurt him a few times and he looked at me and I realized, 'This is a different fight … this guy … somebody lied.' I hit him in the side real hard. He just covered up and went back to the ropes."*
>
> —George Foreman

Round 7.

Foreman, still seeking the one-punch knockout, wears down. His energy expended, the heat, the humidity, the exhaustion all take their toll.

Ali taunts him: *"George, is that all you've got?"*

It was.

Ali survives the storm.

A fatigued Foreman now faces an opponent with reserves of energy. Now, in complete control, Ali bursts to life; a devastating flurry of powerful punches that Foreman is too exhausted to withstand. It ends in the eighth round. The unbreakable Foreman falls broken—a knockout victory shocking the world.

> *"That right hand was the fastest punch I've ever been hit with. Never been hit so fast. It was like he was a lightweight. I didn't even see it coming. I waited, my corner told me to hold it, I jumped up, the fight was over."*
>
> —George Foreman

~~~

Survive the Storm

Ali's lesson is powerful: *Patience. Restraint. Reserve energy. Delay reacting.*

This applies to *so many* facets of life. New social trends. New business strategies. The latest investment craze. Hyped ideas in which "*everyone's on board,*" be it at work, home—everywhere. The human animal is prone to social momentum, getting caught up in the fever of sudden, swift change and not wanting to "*miss the boat.*"

Discipline yourself. **Time reveals truth**.

The best reaction is *no reaction*. Stand back. Slow down. *Observe.*

During accelerated change, emotion suffocates logic. It's the energy of something exciting, something new that will cause perfectly rational people to invest half their life savings in a "*sure-to-work*" investment that ultimately destroys their financial security. To compromise their values for the sake of the crowd. To abandon their better judgement. To commit to a social movement that, in time, proves to be ridiculous. *If everyone else is gaining, I don't want to miss out. If so many people are on board, they must be right.*

Wrong.

Change—and *perceived* opportunity—are coming. In time, energy, resources, and emotion, others will overinvest in it—or overreact against it.

Not you.

The dust will settle. The tide will recede.

While others deplete themselves in the firestorm, you stand back—observe; watch; *wait*. In time, the hype will die down. And when it does—you, with discipline and objectivity, reassess the landscape. You avoid the battle of the ego which, after taking an early position, seeks to defend its choice in the face of mounting contrary evidence. You avoid the internal battle not to be proven "*wrong.*"

The resources others have burned you hold in reserve. When the true nature of change reveals itself, **then** *you gauge the opportunity.* **Then,** *you assess its* *worth*. The next "big thing" is just around the corner. You now know what to do—when the crowd starts running toward it, you don't join them. You don't run in the other direction.

You do *nothing*.

Had Ali entered the fray as expected, he would have been destroyed. He watched, and waited, with pained patience and unwavering discipline.

When the time was right, *he unleashed hell.*

You must do the same.

The next storm is coming. *Time reveals truth.*

Let it.

> *"Dignity of human nature requires that we must face the storms of life."*
> —Mahatma Gandhi

Game of Thrones: Finish Strong

***Game of Thrones,* Season Four.**

Tyrion Lannister is found guilty of a crime he did not commit: poisoning King Joffrey. He chooses *trial by combat;* the Viper vs. the Mountain. Tyrion is doomed to die should the Viper fall. For the Viper, the stakes are personal: the Mountain slaughtered his sister and her children years ago. *Now is the time for vengeance.*

After an intense, pitched battle The Viper knocks down The Mountain. He *could* end the battle with a killing blow at this moment. Defying common sense and logic, he opts not to. The Viper begins pacing around his fallen foe:

> *"Mr. Mountain. My name is Inigo Montoya. You killed my Father.*
> *Prepare to die."*

Still incapacitated, The Mountain lies vulnerable; oblivious. Still, no finishing blow:

> *"I have knocked you down. And now that I have knocked you down, I have*
> *a few things to say that are very important. And because they are very*
> *important, I am going to say them."*

The Mountain remains motionless—a defeated heap. Never has an opponent been easier to finish; with almost no effort the battle could be won. Naturally, The Viper continues:

"… There's more. I am giving you a new name; you are no longer The Mountain.
You are the Viper's Bitch.
I want to hear you say, "I am the Viper's Bitch."
Say it."

After seventeen minutes of dialogue, The Mountain recovers his wits. With a swift sweep of the arm, The Viper is knocked onto his back.

"… Oops."

The Mountain jams his thumb deep into The Viper's eye sockets.

"How did this happen?"

The Mountain smashes The Viper's skull like overripe melon.

Additional oratory by The Viper suspended, as it requires a face.

You've seen this before—if not through this story, through countless others. When it's time to finish, **finish.** Turn off the showmanship. Skip the pageantry. Don't gloat. Don't savor an unsealed victory. Without closure, *nothing* matters. If you overextend the campaign. If you set a bookend without placing the other. If you contemplate. Slow down. Look back. Hesitate. *You lose.*

Define the endpoint. Get there. Get it done. End it. The final chapter is *always* the most important; the story is pointless without it.

How many get so close—and *almost* made it.

That's *their* story. It isn't yours.

Finish strong.

"Some men give up their designs when they have almost reached the goal; While others, on the contrary, obtain a victory by exerting, at the last moment, more vigorous efforts than ever before."

—Herodotus

Fahrenheit 451: The Enemy Within

"Fahrenheit 451: the temperature at which book paper catches fire, and burns."

Ray Bradbury's dystopian masterpiece continues to captivate audiences over 65 years later; it is the rare story that becomes *more relevant* as time goes by. More prophecy than entertainment, *Fahrenheit 451* envisions a society ignorantly planting the seeds of its own destruction. The enemy is not *out there*—

The enemy is within.

Thanks to the precedent Bradbury set, dystopian literature and film remain a captivating genre. Then and now, audiences are hungry for stories depicting a future world destroyed through humanity's carelessness.

In Bradbury's future, firemen no longer put out fires, but search for and destroy illegal literature. Books, and the ideas they represent, are deemed too damaging in the emotions they stir within society. All are banned. Free thinking and knowledge, the future government posits, are not the answer to society's problems—*but the cause of them.*

Our protagonist is fireman Guy Montag, tasked with destroying all remaining books. Guy believes his work is critical, protecting the future of humanity by eradicating its most destructive resource. Guy believes the enemy is *out there*—ignorant that society's greatest danger isn't in propagating ideas, but destroying them. Unaware, like the Government he serves, that he is the real enemy.

Inspired by Clarisse, his neighbor and an outcast, Guy challenges his own beliefs. The world being built is not the promised utopia. His wife, like many others, is addicted to pills—at one point attempting to take her own life. Families are spellbound by their household's *parlor wall*, which provides numbing entertainment to the masses. Life is hollow; meaningless.

A trove of literature is discovered in a woman's house, resulting in the home's burning. The woman will not leave—choosing death over the loss of knowledge her books' destruction represents. Compelled by the woman's conviction, Guy steals a book. Soon, Guy is devouring literature, hungry for enlightenment. Guy's eyes are now open—he understands that destroying books ultimately destroys society. And by propagating their destruction, he is the real enemy.

Guy tells his wife Mildred what is transpiring. Unwilling to abandon what society has taught her, she turns Guy in. He is called to destroy yet another home: *his*. In defiance, he kills Captain Beatty, who, in despair, sought death after once avidly reading books, and now serving their destruction.

Guy escapes, finding a group whose members each serve as the memory keepers for a book they've memorized. The inevitability of society's self-destructive ignorance comes to fruition: The city is destroyed through nuclear annihilation. Time passes. Armed with the gift of knowledge, the exiles return to rebuild society.

Fahrenheit 451. The future Government is its own worst enemy, resulting in society's total destruction. Guy, too, was his own worst enemy through his blind support of the tragic book-burning cause. Ultimately, Guy awakened, fully exposed to the hard truth: the real enemy is not out there—*the real enemy is within*.

Like Guy Montag, we too must awaken to this reality. *Our greatest enemy is ourselves*.

~~~

There's a hero and villain within each of us. One that says, *"Never stop chasing the dream;"* the other says, *"Why bother?"*

For the despondent, the excuses and limitations have been internalized. The external forces given permission to suffocate them do just that. They succumb to the side that sees no point or purpose in anything—sedating themselves from this perceived *"reality"* with alcohol, drugs, and worthless *"just-passing-the-time"* pursuits.

There are no distractions loud enough to overcome this truth: a mind, body, and soul stagnant in pursuit of its greatest purpose will atrophy. There's no amount of counseling, self-help books, medication, or gurus that will replace the void left by not answering our highest calling. Misery finds those unwilling to put their aspirations to action.

Again: *A mind, body, and soul stagnant in pursuit of its greatest purpose will atrophy.*

The optimist and the pessimist, latent in everyone, are two parts of a whole. There is an altruist and narcissist in each of us. There's an advocate; there's a detractor. You cannot control their existence—but you *can* control their dominance.

Think of those you know who speak harshly of themselves. Who constantly vocalize a lack of confidence and capability. That the world, and everyone in it, conspire against them. That life is unfair, and—had they only been given better circumstances—*what a marvel they could have become. What wonders they could have accomplished … if only.*

For us, this trait is tiresome when it dominates others. For them, this trait is devastating in its self-destructiveness. Nothing will stifle pursuing your highest calling more than vocalizing these pseudo-excuses. You get what you claim. This is unseen by *so many.*

For every conscious thought, *hundreds of thousands* of unconscious thoughts occur. Our minds are built for congruency—seeking confirmation of the beliefs we consciously claim. The harmony of thought, action, and outcome are inherent in each of us. The beliefs you consciously feed set your unconscious mind on fire in pursuit.

The first step in overcoming the enemy within us: acknowledging the two sides of ourselves—positive and negative. Awareness of this: *the one we feed will thrive*. We are now aware.

The second step: *claiming our outcome*. In word and thought, paint a visual description of your ultimate goals. Say them out loud the moment you wake up; make them the final spoken words before going to bed. *Share your goals with others, and ask them theirs*. Write your goals down. Put them where they are seen daily. Write them on your bathroom mirror. Write them on an index card on your car dashboard. Make them the wallpaper on your phone. *Immerse yourself in your written goals daily*.

The third step: memorize three quotes, scriptures, or sayings that inspire you.

Self-doubt will creep in. *Combat this*. Every time it does, speak your quotes out loud. This isn't "*spiritual*"; this is practical. We manifest what we vocalize. Put this principle to work and watch your pessimism descend as your confidence ascends. Every time we stifle the negative voice, the vacant space is filled with the positive.

Be unyielding; *every* negative thought is immediately confronted with a positive claim. We are going to feed ourselves inspiration—not dejection. Again, the healthy mind demands congruency. In claiming your dream, your mind—in its entirety—goes to work setting that dream to action. Nothing is more powerful.

So few are aware of the truth: Like Ray Bradbury's dystopian future, we are our own worst enemy. *But no more*. We were, once—but no longer. Guy Montag awakens. *As have we*. The enemy within claims it's all pointless. That enemy is dead. It is done. It is broken. It is defeated.

From this moment on, we feed the positive aspirations within us. We speak our dreams to life. We combat negativity when it surfaces. We go to war with self-doubt. We claim our goals as *already ours*.

In doing so, a new truth replaces the old: For you, **anything is possible**.

It starts here and now.

"Man is his own worst enemy."

—Marcus Tullius Cicero

Addiction: The Real Killer

We are killing ourselves. The number-one cause of death for people over 50: *heart disease*. The number-one cause of death below 50: *overdose*.

How did we get here?

~~~

Percocet. Vicodin. Lortab.

In the late 1990s, a movement begins intending to help those with chronic pain. The rate of opioid prescriptions soar; their addictive qualities not fully understood. As opioid abuse becomes an epidemic, restrictions are implemented to reduce the drug's abuse. Many who had easy access to painkillers suddenly have none. To feed their addiction, the addict buys pain pills illegally. The number of pills once purchased for a modest prescription copay now cost *hundreds* of dollars.

The cost is not sustainable. *The addiction will be fed.*

Heroin.

Like painkillers, heroin is an opioid—though many times more potent, *and many times more deadly*. The economics compel the painkiller addict to seek out heroin, as it costs far less than the painkillers it can replace. *The next opioid epidemic arrives:*

Fentanyl.

Fentanyl, a synthetic opiate, is FDA-approved for patients who've developed a resistance to painkillers. *It is 50 times more potent than heroin.*

The opioid epidemic marches on. Deadlier options continue to arrive, at lower cost to acquire. The overdose death rate tragically accelerates.

~~~

The *prescription painkiller to Fentanyl* narrative parallels the nature of addiction itself: It never starts with an awareness of the devastation to come. It starts modestly. The addict does not see the path ahead: What he or she believes will be a one-time use leads directly to the grave. Opioids are only one of countless drugs ruining lives—*and ending them.*

Alcoholism, addiction.

Substance abuse remains the monster in the corner no one wants to talk about. The discussion needs to happen. ***Now.*** Take measure of alcoholism and addiction. Friends, family, loved ones. Those who struggle. *Those we have lost.*

Now think of yourself. Substance abuse does *everything it can* to convince you *there's no problem.* Stand back. Go to the mirror. Analyze. Assess. Consider your life. Consider your vices. Without anger, without disappointment, entirely free from emotion—*what do you see?*

Is it time for change?

Is there a habit in your life that, if you knew a loved one was experiencing, *you would do anything you could to help them*? If your children were struggling with what you are struggling with, *what would you say to them?* **You would not tell them to ignore a habit that is killing them**. You *must* hold yourself to the same standard.

For you, that habit may be drug or alcohol abuse. But it might be something else. The destruction wrought by addiction goes beyond the obvious sources. Food, sex, relationships: When a person's involvement with these things becomes unhealthy, they can consume that person's life, drain their potential, and lead them to hurt or neglect the people around them.

Work is no exception. The term *workaholic* is no joke. Some develop an unhealthy dependency on the rush of professional success. Others immerse themselves in their work so they might become numb to problems in other areas of their lives. You do not need to be enslaved to drugs or alcohol to struggle with the same psychological vulnerabilities faced by those with these addictions.

You would do **anything** in your power to help a loved one struggling with such a problem—a loved one torn away by vice from the things that *really* give their life meaning. Understand: That is **exactly** how you need to treat yourself.

~~~

Alcohol. Vicodin. OxyContin. Cocaine. Heroin. Duragesic. Demerol. Morphine. Valium. Xanax. Ambien. Zoloft. Dexadrine. Ritalin. Concerta. Adderall. And countless others.

~~~

The real killer is our inaction.

Face yourself.

If you need help, *stop looking through the window*. Look in the mirror. Face the hard truth that is haunting you—the desperate need for help; the stranger reflected back, *pleading* for change.

The real killer is our inaction.

Reject the concept that your struggles are weakness. _They are not._ You have a disease. You need treatment.

The real killer is our inaction.

I will tell you what strength is _not: trying to do it alone._ Strength is getting help. _You are not alone._

Substance Abuse and Mental Health Services Administration; free, confidential help.

This is the moment. _Now is the time._

1.800.662.4357

~~~

Family and friends of alcoholics and addicts, I tell you this: after their recovery, they will have endless gratitude toward those who helped them face their deadly reality. It isn't easy to do. _It is the right thing to do._ It is the very definition of walking in love, which ultimately wins.

For the non-addicts who feel they fully understand addiction: _You do not understand._ It is not possible. Their disease is theirs—_not yours._ Act from care and concern, but not from a false belief of _"understanding"._

You do not. You cannot. And hopefully—with God's grace—_you never will._

> _"So do not fear, for I am with you; do not be dismayed, for I am your God. I will strengthen you and help you; I will uphold you with my righteous right hand."_
> **—Isaiah 41:10**

In Loving Memory

~~~

Jimi Hendrix

—

Janis Joplin

—

Prince

—

John Bonham

—

Frida Kahlo

—

Tom Petty

—

Judy Garland

—

Lenny Bruce

—

Chris Farley

—

Jim Morrison

—

Edgar Allan Poe

—

Sigmund Freud

—

John Belushi

—

Philip Seymour Hoffman

—

Jean-Michel Basquiat

—

Chyna

—

Coco Chanel

—

Sid Vicious

—

Cory Monteith

—

George Best

—

Brian Jones

—

Layne Staley

—

Keith Moon

—

Bon Scott

—

Truman Capote

—

Paul Gauguin

—

Mitch Hedberg

—

Chet Baker

—

Dana Plato

—

Alan Ladd

—

Frankie Lymon

—

Louisa May Alcott

—

Heath Ledger

—

Brad Renfro

—

Daniel Webster

—

Elvis Presley

—

Edie Sedgwick

—

Rob Pilatus

—

Whitney Houston

—

Dorothy Dandridge

—

Inger Stevens

—

Dorothy Kilgallen

—

Kenneth Williams

—

Hillel Slovak

—

Diana Churchill

—

Guru Dutt

—

Anissa Jones

—

Neal Cassady

—

Lester Bangs

—

Brendan Behan

—

John Tyndall

—

Jeanne Eagels

—

Amy Winehouse

—

Ike Turner

—

Peaches Geldof

—

Paula Yates

—

David Ruffin

—

Bruce Lee

—

John Entwistle

—

Keith Whitley

—

Nick Drake

—

Thomas Kinkade

—

Gram Parsons

—

Christina Onassis

—

Brian Epstein

—

Kevin DuBrow

—

Jeff Hanneman

—

Pier Angeli

—

Tim Buckley

—

Domino Harvey

"The only person you are destined to become is the person you decide to be."
—Ralph Waldo Emerson

SECTION VII
CHANGE THE FRAME

Viktor E. Frankl: Change the Frame

Viktor E. Frankl. World-renowned best-selling author. Neurologist. Psychiatrist.

Holocaust survivor.

For three years, Frankl survived the torture and starvation of Nazi concentration camps. The horror of the Holocaust took an unspeakable toll: He survived the death of his wife, his family, and the majority of his fellow inmates. Frankl speaks of the rare instance when a prisoner was rewarded a cigarette for exemplary work—a cigarette that could be traded for a cup of thin broth. A cigarette—*a single cigarette*—whose trade value may literally mean the difference between life and death. The prisoner resigned to smoking their cigarette was not enjoying a hard-earned reprieve but, as Frankl tragically observes, bidding a final farewell to the world by choosing not to trade the cigarette for soup. Unable to find meaning or hope in unimaginable suffering, these prisoners abandoned their will to carry on.

Frankl's lesson: In the darkest of times, in the most horrible of places—to give up on yourself, to give up on *meaning,* is to die. Frankl's own suffering, his choice day after day of soup over a cigarette, reveals the human ability—in mind, body, soul, and spirit—*to endure.* His story tells you, I, and all who follow, *"You shall overcome. And the reward for enduring your struggle is that you will change the world."*

Frankl survived the Holocaust—but that was only one step in his journey. After his experience, he gifted the world a life-changing concept: **logotherapy**.

*"Rather than power or pleasure, **logotherapy** is founded upon the belief that striving to find **meaning** in life is the primary, most powerful motivating and driving force in humans."*

Logotherapy opens the path from tragedy into triumph, leading us from our darkest days to our greatest victories.

Frankl demonstrates logotherapy in action. An elderly client visits him for counsel, unable to escape the depression of losing his beloved wife two years prior. Frankl responds with a question: What if she had to survive *your* passing? The man relays how much suffering this would have caused her. In this moment, the client sees the value in his suffering: By surviving, he has spared the love of his life an unbearable burden. He sees that each day lived without his wife is a tribute to his love for her; each day in silent mourning rich in meaning and purpose, an act of commemoration of her life. His tragedy is thus transformed into triumph.

Frankl experienced an atrocity, and he used what he learned to invent a form of therapy that helped countless people overcome life's greatest challenges. The grieving client had one of the most heartbreaking experiences an individual can, and he learned to see it as a final gift and tribute to his wife.

They survived by **reframing**. You don't need to experience a life-shattering tragedy to learn from their example. Reframing is the most powerful tool we have to cope with problems, big and small—and leaders *must* master it to break through the ceiling of *good* to become truly great.

It starts with meaning.

It isn't power. It isn't privilege. It is *meaning* that fills the existential hole within us. It is that grand *something* that's missing for many people, but that is required for our ultimate purpose to be fulfilled.

Tragedy is part of life. The hardest part. *None are exempt.* We're going to see our way from tragedy to meaning. We're going to see ourselves not as victims of cruel external circumstances—but as warriors whose suffering is no barrier to our purpose. Warriors empowered by a message, and a belief, that can change not only our lives, but the lives of those around us.

The storms will keep coming. You will survive. You will thrive. Your suffering is also strength. You can use that strength to pursue something much bigger and far better: the manifestation of your ultimate purpose.

~~~

Many Holocaust survivors see their experiences differently than Frankl did. To them, there is no silver lining to the darkest depths of human evil. Many might object to the notion of finding something positive in great suffering, and if you have experienced unthinkable tragedy, you might agree. *I am not trying to change your mind.* Who am I to tell you the meaning of your suffering?

Understand: You might object to the "silver lining" theory. These objections are legitimate. And you can still implement Frankl's theory in your life, to the benefit of yourself and those around you. *Allow me to explain the "how."*

Frankl's story and that of his grieving client share a common thread. Both men coped by doing two things: 1) Looking to the future, and 2) Contributing something to the world that's bigger than themselves. Frankl alleviated human suffering through a therapy that helps deeply traumatized people when nothing else does. The husband came to understand his grief as a gift and tribute to the person he loved most.

You may always see your tragedy as a tragedy. For you, changing the frame might mean adjusting your understanding of your life as a whole—the story you tell yourself of your own journey; the narrative that gives you meaning. Your tragedy is not your defining experience. It is one small component of a life that will be remembered for its contributions to the world, contributions so great that even the most immense suffering will be diminished.

Frankl moved *onward* to contribute something meaningful to humanity. The Holocaust is one part of his story—a fundamental part—but first, he was an accomplished author. A neurologist. A psychiatrist. And *then*, he was a survivor. You, too, are more than a survivor. Embracing that means focusing on others. Recognizing yourself as a positive contributor to the world around you. And most of all—*finding meaning by thinking big*. Start by sharing your story. Voice your triumph over your trials. Show others what can be overcome. Show them that life isn't about avoiding the fight—*that life is the fight*.

My choice to explain this truth through a therapist's story is no coincidence. Therapy helps *everyone*. Whether riding high or smashed against the rocks, *speak with a therapist*. Lives are changed—and saved—through therapeutic techniques that help us change the frame. You are not alone on this journey.

I proudly share my story, my discovery of meaning, with you. It is not an atrocity. It is *nothing* like Frankl's suffering in the Holocaust. But like Frankl, I used reframing to find meaning and the power to endure. So too can you.

~~~

The breakdown found me.

In trying to be everything to everyone, I became nothing to anyone. Broken by the belief that perfection is not only obtainable, but necessary. A prisoner of my own disillusionment; that, in my life, the only direction anything would ever move was up.

With open arms, the hospital—and the reality it represented—awaited me. Seven days in a mental health facility, overlooking the stunning Southern California coast. The contrast of the hospital with that coast—that *postcard* sunset—*it should have been depressing*.

But it wasn't. It was *liberating*.

Mental health. The psychiatric ward. *The great leveler.* We were all equals in that place. I one of so many. Matching only in hospital gowns; nothing more. On the surface, no two alike.

A schoolteacher who had fallen off the wagon. A husband who had lost his wife—who couldn't live in a world in which she was no longer living, who couldn't be the father his children needed. A trust fund kid battling the needle. A privileged wife and mother who felt she was standing on a cliff, with nothing ahead but oblivion.

At the cafeteria table, we talked. We laughed. We played cards and drank orange juice from small plastic containers. We worked on a puzzle depicting Old Route 66.

No two *remotely* alike.

~~~

And so came a defining experience of my life. I grew more in those seven days than in the seven years before them. A lesson in living, in human nature; in humility. *I would change nothing.*

The lesson was acceptance. Seeing the same struggles, the same suffering in every face at the table—and the same potential for endurance and triumph—revealed to me that my pain, which I had thought was unique in my dark trial, was anything but. My companions were patients. They were also mothers, fathers, siblings. Leaders, employees, mentors. Contributors, all. Their challenges did not detract from their lives' meaning, nor did their accomplishments erase their challenges.

I deal now in reality. The silent companion, dormant, is still there. The neurons and synapses fire differently for me; the chemicals chart unfamiliar pathways. No degree of optimism will change it—only acceptance of what is.

My surrogate family. Us together at the table—that sunset. Part of me is still there. *The **best** part of me.*

The part that now understands. That is willing to accept what *is* instead of *what ought to be*. Willing to turn that reality into strength, into release—into oxygen. Transforming what could be an anchor into power. Driven to let you know that *every* life has meaning. To let you know that pursuing the false God called *perfection* will destroy you. It does not exist.

To let you know that life is beauty. And life is pain. And everything in between. That no matter the scope of your struggle, you are *never* alone. The future is yours—and yet to be written. And through it all, you will rise once again.

I stood. Then, I broke down. Then, I stood once again—only, having found meaning within and beyond the struggle, I stood taller.

As it shall be for you.

You *cannot* change the picture. You *cannot* change the past. You *can* change its meaning. You *can* change the frame. Do it. *There's so much waiting for you on the other side.* Now is the time. Take your trials. Gather your tragedies. *All of them.*

Now, change the frame.

A Personal Farewell: Turn the Page

And so, as foretold by the Hero's Journey, we return to our world. We return to our lives, taking what we've learned to transform the world of our colleagues, family, friends—ourselves.

Whoever you are, wherever you are, whenever you are—these principles are timeless. These principles are *yours*. You have the tools to make a true impact. You have the drive to build Heaven on Earth. *Sculpt your masterpiece.*

Three words to guide you: *courage, hustle,* and *heart. Courage* to step away from comfort toward your highest pursuit. *Hustle* to do so with swift action. *Heart* to do so with relentless resolve.

The first principle is this: Keep perspective. We live in the moment, so focused on the *here and now*, often oblivious to the larger picture. Too close to all of it, we lose sight of a simple truth: *This too shall pass.* No matter the challenge—*you will endure.*

Reject the circumstances you allow to hold you back. *It is a decision.* Some sit forever, contemplating who had it better, worse; the disadvantages born into—the opportunities ungiven. Those self-imposed obsessions suffocate their potential. *Not you.* You are unchained from your past. There are only the remains of *this* day—*and all the days to follow.*

Let this be our guiding principle:

Onward.

Life will knock you down.

Onward.

You will fail.

Onward.

You will fall.

But when you fall—*you choose the direction*. Fall toward your aspirations. *Fall toward your purpose*. Whether in Heaven or the gutter: Onward. *"Down and out"* will try to claim you. *"Up and out"* is your decision.

Understand this: life is messy; at times, broken—at times, complicated. Any life worth living—at some point—will face seemingly unbearable circumstances. If you aren't failing, you aren't growing. You aren't taking the chances true living requires. *This too shall pass.* Life will humble you. *Let it.* When it's easy: Onward. When it's hard: Onward. Locked onto your full potential, *always* facing True North.

Live life this way, *and I promise you will get there.*

A day is coming.

On that day, you will look back at your life, and see a story has been written. That, somehow, the glory and the pain and the triumphs and the tragedies were all part of something larger; a grand narrative defining the purpose of your life. *Make that purpose the relentless pursuit of your potential.*

Onward: The Art of Leadership. *The Art of Living.* Every moment the story of your life is being written.

And you hold the pen.

~~~

Goodbye to you. Goodbye—but only for a time. The page now turns. One chapter ends. The next begins.

We have something wonderful in common, you and I.

For both of us,

this is not the end…

This is the beginning.

—Mark Joseph Huckabee